WHY IS EVERYONE SMILING?

WHY IS EVERYONE SMILING?

The Secret Behind Passion, Productivity, and Profit

PAUL SPIEGELMAN

Brown Books Publishing Group

Dallas, Texas

WHY IS EVERYONE SMILING?

The Secret Behind Passion, Productivity, and Profit

Manufactured in the United States of America

For information, please contact:

Brown Books Publishing Group

16200 North Dallas Parkway, Suite 170

Dallas, Texas 75248

www.brownbooks.com

972-381-0009

A New Era in Publishing™

ISBN-13: 978-1-933285-80-1

ISBN-10: 1-933285-80-X

LCCN: 2007925864

1 2 3 4 5 6 7 8 9 10

Dedication

To my ever-growing family—my lovely wife, Teresa, and beautiful children, Jordan and Dylan; to my brother, Mark, for his talent and passion, and to our brother, Barry, whose life ended far too early but whose smile will never leave us; to my parents, whose values are what we still live by today; and to my Beryl family, each and every one of whom has touched and inspired me.

Table of Contents

Foreword

by Bo Burlingham

Every now and then, I run into companies that have something very special going for them. It's not just that they're successful in a traditional business sense, although they always are. They also have a certain intangible, indefinable quality that you can sense as soon as you set foot in the business, or spend time around its employees, or talk to its customers and suppliers. There's a magnetism, a power of attraction, that draws people to the company and makes them feel a strong desire to be connected to it.

I first began to notice companies with this special quality in the early 1980s, after I joined the staff of *Inc.* magazine and got to know some of the terrific young businesses that were revitalizing the U.S. economy back then. Their names are familiar today: Apple Computer, Patagonia, Intel, Southwest Airlines, Quad/Graphics, Microsoft, Nucor Steel, Ben & Jerry's, Federal Express, and so on. I didn't have a name for the quality back then, but I do now. It's what I call *mojo*, and I think of it as the business equivalent of charisma. When a leader has charisma, you want to follow him or her. When a company has charisma, you want to be associated with it—buy from it, sell to it, work for it, wear its t-shirts and baseball caps, read books and articles about it, recommend it to friends, whatever.

In doing research for my book *Small Giants: Companies That Choose to Be Great Instead of Big*, I studied fourteen companies that radiated mojo, and I tried to figure out where it came from, what they did to generate it. I wondered, in particular, how it was related to something I had noticed about the owners of these companies, namely, their common conviction that business could be a means for experiencing some of the best things in life—exciting challenges, camaraderie, compassion, hope, community, a sense of purpose, feelings of accomplishment. The closer I looked, the clearer it became that this conviction was intimately tied to the companies' mojo. In effect, the owners had organized their companies so that they and their employees could experience these good things on a regular basis.

I have since come across many other companies that fit the small giants mold. Some of them fit it so well that I have caught myself wishing I had encountered them a couple of years earlier, so that I could have included them in my book. The Beryl Companies falls squarely into that exclusive group. Like other small giants, Beryl enjoyed the kind of success early on that brought with it numerous opportunities to expand, as well as relentless pressure to grow as fast as possible and get as big as possible. But Paul Spiegelman and his brothers decided to resist that pressure, keep ownership and control inside the business, and focus instead on building a company that would be the best at what it did—connecting people to healthcare—with an engaged and loyal workforce that had the same passion for the business, its mission, its vision, and its values as the owners.

And they succeeded. Over the past twenty years, Paul and his colleagues have created an incredibly vibrant culture, based on open book communication, continuous learning, personal growth, and unabashed fun. You don't need me to explain how they did it, or to recount all the struggles they went through to build the extraordinary business they have today. Paul tells the story eloquently and insightfully in the pages that follow. But perhaps I can add a little context.

What Paul presents here is a thoroughly absorbing account of how one great company implemented some timeless business principles and thereby rose to the top of its industry. Along the way, he provides countless take-away lessons for other companies. Not that he has some sort of recipe for success. I don't believe there is a recipe for building a Small Giant. But it always helps to know what you're striving for, and—as role models go—Beryl is as good as they come. It has all the characteristics of the other small giants I have seen, in particular the five key characteristics that give them their mojo. Those are: (1) owners and leaders with a clear understanding of who they are, what they want out of business, and why; (2) deep connections to the community in which they do business; (3) close, personal, one-on-one relationships with customers and suppliers; (4) a culture of intimacy, built around "caring for people in the totality of their lives," to borrow a phrase from Herb Kelleher of Southwest Airlines; and (5) owners and leaders who love what their companies do, who are so passionate about it that they want everyone they come into contact with to feel the same way.

That said, it's also important to take note of the differences in the paths that Beryl and the other companies have taken to wind up in more or less the same place. When you think about it, that's not so surprising, considering the infinite number of variables in business—from the personalities of people involved, to the nature of the industry, to all the unforeseeable twists and turns of fortune. It's a reminder that every company has to find its own way. No formula exists for making small giants, and if you're looking for one, you're going to be disappointed.

But while there isn't a formula, there are certain higher laws in business, as I learned long ago from my erstwhile co-author and mentor Jack Stack—the CEO of SRC Holdings and pioneer of open-book management. You find out what those laws are either by your own process of trial and error, or by studying the trials and errors, as well as the successes, of other people. And therein lies the true value of this book. It is obvious from what Paul Spiegelman and his colleagues have accomplished that they have discovered the higher laws of business. By sharing what he's learned, Paul has done us all a great service. I just hope you will feel as inspired by his story as I have been.

—Bo Burlingham
Editor-at-Large, *Inc.* magazine
Author of
Small Giants: Companies That Choose to Be Great Instead of Big

Acknowledgements

Most of the people whom I would thank for helping me shape the thoughts I convey through these pages are mentioned in the book, because my story is really about how others have impacted my life. For direct involvement in my book, my special thanks and friendship to Craig Hanley who helped shape my thoughts in a way that readers could hear my voice. I also want to thank everyone on the team at Brown Books, who took a rookie author through the paces with great passion and patience.

Much of the essence of this book comes from the personal stories of Beryl coworkers that have touched me over the years. This is really about them and for them. Many are mentioned in the book, but I owe my gratitude to the thousands with whom we have worked over the last twenty-two years. With each new relationship, I learned something new about myself and tried to improve as a leader.

Without a formal board of directors or advisors, I have come to trust a small circle of mentors who have guided me through days of joy and days of insecurity and indecision. If not for their support, I would have achieved far less. Though he was busy building a multibillion dollar company, Rick Scott took a chance on three brothers who had little more than passion and a commitment to succeed. But over ten years ago, he chose us and invested in us, and for that we'll be forever grateful. He continues to be a trusted advisor who has been willing to give me his time and his straightforward advice.

I have also had the pleasure of working with Pete Lakey, who has brought his years of experience and wisdom to my small world, but has made a huge impact on me. He has taken the time to mentor not only me, but has built trusted relationships with every member of our management team. There isn't a situation that comes up that Pete can't help solve with a story, an article, a tape or a book.

Mark Lefko is another source of great inspiration. I'll never forget the first time that Mark took Barry and me on a day-long strategic retreat. We spent our time in the Malibu mountains, ate organic food, and took a hike. Mark has always helped me to stay focused on what is important outside of work and to continue to pursue my passions.

Other advisors, like Rubin Turner and Paul Devore have always been there for me at any time of day or night. I consider myself very lucky that these and other special people have been willing to help me.

I want to thank Pat Benner, our former CFO who made the important life choice to stop commuting to Dallas and stay closer to his wife and young girls in Colorado. But Pat taught me about many things, including how to build discipline and accountability in a small business that lacked much formal structure.

Life and business are both about the same thing—relationships. I can only thank my parents for instilling in my brothers and me the importance of family. Because when it is all said and done, and I reflect about the purpose of life and the purpose of business, it is really just about family. I am very fortunate that I have a beautiful family to come home to every night. But I also have a family that I get to see every day at Beryl. I get the same reception that I do at home—open arms and smiles. Our business is about raising a family of people who are passionate about what they do every day. When I hear the common refrain from coworkers that "I love to come to work in the morning," then I know I've done my job.

Preface

As this book prepares to go to print, I am dressed in a Spanish bullfighter's outfit and roller skates. My chief operating officer, a rangy six foot four outdoorsman, is dressed like a harem girl in sky blue silk pants, a heavily-padded bikini top and a veil. For the last half hour, while a disco ball spins overhead and Michael Jackson sings "Don't Stop Till You Get Enough," Lance and I have been clumsily attempting a synchronized dance number on skates in a rink we rented near the office. It's a skit for a video that will play at The Beryl Companies' upcoming holiday dinner.

Our mutual inability to stay on our feet keeps cracking up the camera crew. I've done so many of these comic videos by now I'm surprised that I can't keep a straight face either. But that's a good sign. It means our coworkers will probably enjoy the program. And during the dinner a week later, they do, immensely.

I am not a full-time roller-skating matador. I'm a typically driven CEO of a very successful small company that has made a conscious decision to stay small. We focus on quality incremental growth because we don't think dynamic expansion can improve the results of our unique culture strategy. In an industry where turnover usually averages 80 to 90 percent, ours is 17 percent. Our client retention rate is 95 percent, and we charge significantly more for our services than the industry average. Oddly enough, the skating bullfighter skit will help reinforce these numbers.

After twenty years of very hands-on experience, I wrote this book to offer some pointers on how to turn a small, privately-owned business into a premium provider that delivers a higher level of profit. These tactics will be especially helpful to people who own and manage "commodity" businesses that tradition-ally compete on price. Whether you sell coat hangers or creative graphic design, if your customers focus more on cost than any other factor, you are running a commodity business.

I also wrote the book because I'd like to see fellow business leaders stop treating their coworkers like commodities. Leaders should more fully understand the profound impact they can have on the lives of the people who work with them. And every business owner should realize how personally fulfilling it can be to treat coworkers exceptionally well and develop them continuously. We've documented the financial rewards of this approach at The Beryl Companies for two decades. The strategy now motivates a workforce of diverse backgrounds, education, and experience.

I don't pretend to be a world-class management visionary, but it doesn't take a prophet to see serious fault lines developing in the American corporate landscape. Number-driven executive teams focus on complex global market trends, but forget common sense fundamentals and a basic sense of humanity. The result? Far too many of the new hires at Beryl describe immensely demoralizing environments at former places of employment. And epidemic low morale is no surprise in an age of spectacular and endless executive scandals.

Beryl's culture story proves two things: when you treat your people like true contributors, it does the business tremendous good; when you focus your business on solid values, it benefits both the community and the economy. The best new model for the future of American business is smart, small, ethical companies willing to make long-term investments in a loyal local workforce.

Many management books today seem to want to shock some life back into companies that are just about to flatline. The authors describe the worst possible strains of organizational dysfunction and then pretend that sets of snappy generic formulae will solve these problems equally well for every business under the sun. It's an easy way to make a book, but not a very honest one.

I have tried to present a lot of practical real world tactics, along with a handful of field-tested strategies that should bear fruit for viable small businesses that want to hit their full potential. It's a less dramatic proposition than pulling a doomed operation out of the grave, but probably a more valuable long-term concern for most business owners and managers.

I bet you will walk away with something useful.

CHAPTER ONE:

FROM THE COT TO HOT

I n 2006, The Beryl Companies was the leading customer interaction firm in the U.S. healthcare provider market. *Texas Monthly* magazine had named us one of the best places to work in the state for the second straight year. Profits and revenues were high and climbing, and we didn't have a competitor in sight.

Things had sure changed in twenty years!

In 1985, the whole operation was just three brothers in a tiny conference room that our dad let us take over in his office. We turned this cramped space into a monitoring station for a start-up that provided emergency medical assistance. The inspiration for the company came in 1984 when our grandfather began to suffer from congestive heart failure. My older brother Mark was the technical wizard in the family and was already running a successful alarm system company. When he saw our grandfather in such a vulnerable state, it inspired him to develop an emergency response technology that could help other compromised people.

Mark, my younger brother Barry, and I had always been close. We grew up together in Los Angeles and were trying to figure out a way to go into some kind of business together. When Mark finished his call device prototype, we felt it would make us competitive in the emergency response market. It seemed like a great way to make a lot of people safer and basically make the world a better place. Our grandfather's ordeal had stressed the whole family out, and we knew what other families went through, worrying about loved ones who could suddenly take a dangerous turn for the worse.

Our company, Emergency Response Systems (ERS), was an early entrant in the market. We didn't sell directly to consumers like the company that saturated the airwaves a few years later with the TV ads that featured seniors yelling, "I've fallen . . . and I can't get up!" Instead, we worked directly with hospitals to make sure they could stay in touch with high-risk patients.

In the early days, ERS was the most spartan outfit you could imagine. Fortunately, none of us had any major financial obligations, and we got by on shoestring salaries. To respond to patients who called for help, one of us had to be on duty in the monitoring room around the clock. For the first year and a half, Mark, Barry, and I took turns pulling shifts and never had a day off. Many birthdays and holidays were celebrated right in front of the alert screen.

We had a small client base and emergencies were few and far between. Some weeks we'd only handle one or two calls. To kill time in between, we ate a thousand Domino's pizzas and watched TV. It was super-tedious work, but you always had to be alert and ready to connect a client to healthcare when he or she needed it desperately. There was a cot against the wall that we could stretch out on if we were really exhausted. I will never forget that cot. In my mind, it still symbolizes the spirit of every struggling start-up.

STAYING THE COURSE

THE FACTS OF BUSINESS FINANCE HIT US HARD the day we realized that every emergency device Mark built in my garage was going to cost $250. If we wanted thousands of people to use these things, we were obviously going to need investors. Our ability to raise money was limited from the start. Our dad was a successful attorney, but not a wealthy man. We had no contacts in the investment community. So a buddy of mine from my college days at UCLA and I sat down and wrote a business plan an inch and a half thick.

The idea was to raise $1.2 million in $15,000 increments. We beat the bushes for months, sold one share to a friend of my father, and had to give that check back when everybody else turned us down. It was always the same excuse. Great idea, but you're too young, and the company will never click without an older and wiser management team.

Technically, they had a point. Barry had just graduated from college and I didn't yet have two years under my belt as a lawyer. Mark had proven entrepreneurial talent, but he'd only been running his alarm business for a few years. Nobody could blame the naysayers for their doubts. In a weird way, we owe those doubters a real debt of gratitude. By telling three headstrong young guys that we were bound to fail, they made us more persistent and determined to do things on our own. Nobody would back us, so we accepted the fact that we'd have to chart our own course in the market.

Staying the course was tough. We worked every prospect and opportunity we could identify. A few times, our dad bailed us out with small loans so that we could keep the doors open. It was starting to look like we might have to shut them for good.

IN THE PUBLIC EYE

ONE SATURDAY I WAS WORKING THE MIDNIGHT SHIFT and heard an unusual tapping noise over the receiver. We had patients scattered throughout the greater Los Angeles area, and this call was coming in from Elulia Newsom, a ninety-three-year-old woman who lived in Inglewood. As was our protocol, I tried to talk to her through the speakerphone in her home. For some reason she didn't communicate back to me verbally. All I could hear was faint knocking. These random signals worried me, so I sent paramedics to the address.

They found Elulia locked in a closet and near death. She had been beaten and stabbed repeatedly by an intruder who broke into her home to steal money. Ms. Newsom described the ordeal the next day in a front-page article in the *LA Times*. When the robber tore off the plastic pendant she was wearing around her neck, she claimed it was a "locket" with sentimental value and begged to have it back. The pendant was really the pushbutton alarm that our company supplied. Her attacker threw the pendant into the closet and then shoved Elulia in, wedging the door shut with the bloody knife. For two hours, Ms. Newsom groped around in the bottom of that dark closet. When she finally found the pushbutton device, it activated the speakerphone in our unit and she started banging on the door. That was the noise I heard.

This experience was a milestone for my brothers and me. It felt great to know that the idea we'd dreamed up had actually helped to save a human life in such a dramatic fashion. Naturally, we hoped all the investors who turned us down had a chance to read the article and see the TV news stories. We didn't have much time to gloat. Shortly after this episode, we lucked into the kind of opportunity that seems to pop up for people who work really hard and have good intentions.

I got a lunch invitation from Barbara Wexler, a client of ours who ran the marketing department for Granada Hills Community Hospital. Barbara wanted her hospital to start offering a phone number people could call to get help finding a doctor. I didn't know much about physician referral services, but Barbara said, "Paul, you guys are sitting around in the office twenty-four hours a day, not doing a heck of a lot. What if you put in a phone line and started handling calls for us?" It made no sense to me until she mentioned a monthly retainer fee of three thousand dollars. Suddenly, it made great sense! And two weeks later we were answering calls. Little did we know we were now in the "outsourcing" and "call center" businesses. Nobody had ever heard those words. Now, they are common terms too easily referring to business that is shipped overseas to save money.

Compared to modern data-mining software, our first physician referral system was downright primitive. We'd basically answer the phone and read the names of different doctors off index cards. But it was clear to us right away that every hospital in the country would eventually need to offer this service if it wanted to bond with its community. This side of the business grew rapidly and we were finally making enough money to hire some help. My brothers and I were looking forward to an occasional day off.

PEOPLE WHO NEED PEOPLE

OUR FIRST COWORKER, ANNE RAMSEY, was a charming UCLA drama student who worked as a receptionist in our building. She went on to play Helen Hunt's sister on the Paul Reiser sitcom *Mad About You*. We remember Anne fondly for the crazy outfits she liked to wear to work every day. It was always fun to see what kind of new artsy-grunge look she was into.

Our second coworker was another college student, a personable frat guy who came across as very responsible and trustworthy in his interview. We found out the hard way that he was sneaking his girlfriend into the office during his graveyard shift to help relieve the monotony. When I dropped by the office at two o'clock one morning to pick up some papers, they were so involved they never heard me enter or leave. Fortunately there were no emergency calls on the monitor. We had a pleasant and productive talk about this the next day.

Our third coworker really opened our eyes. During one of his late-night shifts, he was spotted enjoying a meal at the Fat Burger restaurant three blocks down the street from the console he should have been manning. When I explained to him that connecting our callers to healthcare was a matter of life and death, he responded with the rudest two-word expression in the English language. From that day forward, my brothers and I started to take a more serious approach to the critical challenges that managing people can involve. Our mother had many years of experience as a schoolteacher, so she joined the company and trained our coworkers for the next ten years. Her natural warmth in dealing with these trainees set the tone for the culture that would eventually distinguish the company.

LIFE AFTER DEBT

WE SOLD ERS IN 1994 WHEN WE FINALLY FIGURED OUT that the emergency response business would always be too capital-intensive for us. Throughout the late eighties, we had debt-financed the business on a line of credit that we found harder and harder to keep up with. None of us understood the nature of building a relationship with a bank. Our biggest mistake was not keeping our officers up to speed on everything that was happening. One grim day they transferred our account to the "Special Assets Group," which is just a polite name for the collection department.

Our payroll wasn't jeopardized, and we never felt the business was at risk, but we were all ashamed of the rookie errors. It wasn't easy getting out of the doghouse, either. We had to put our heads down and fight our way through the debt steadily and systematically. We never wanted to find ourselves in the same bind again. This wariness revolutionized our operational philosophy. We've been best friends with our bankers ever since and remain one of their most solid customers. We've certainly come a long way from the days when our dad had to bail us out with little loans from his checking account. It's ironic how everybody throws cash at you when you *don't* need it. We get multiple calls a week now from potential backers and spend a lot of time turning money away. In the final analysis, anyway, I'd rather sell to customers than to investors.

Hard work, luck and timing were on our side again in 1995. We won a contract to manage the national physician referral program for Columbia/HCA, the world's largest healthcare company. Definitely the dark horse in this competition, we threw everything we had into crafting an irresistible proposal. The entire management team spent nine months on the pitch, night and day. We gave the client valuable new perspectives on their operation, and they gave us an unlimited budget to build a major new call center in the Dallas area.

It was a dream come true, and it vaulted us into what we considered the big leagues. When construction was finished and my brothers and I walked through the gleaming new facility, we could hardly believe our eyes. The space was big enough for four hundred call advisors and there wasn't a cot or a pizza box in sight.

Three years later, our lives flashed before our eyes when management changes on the client side threatened to kill the whole deal. We ended up buying the assets of the call center on favorable terms and turning it into the platform for a more sophisticated information-based business. We closed our California operations and consolidated everything in Texas.

When my wife and I decided to finally become Texans after seven years of commuting, our friends in Santa Monica and our family thought we'd lost our minds. But we knew the central location and other local assets would help us evolve the company. From a personal standpoint, the move was inevitable. I'd gotten married and had a child, and commuting three days a week didn't make any sense. I needed to be close to my family, the business, and the Beryl family of coworkers. Fortunately, my wife was very understanding and supportive.

Mom wouldn't come, so we had to fire her.

A HOT PROPERTY

BY 2002, THE BUSINESS WAS DOING VERY WELL and had started to attract interest in a market where merger and acquisition activity was at an all-time high. Beryl was never for sale, but we were frequently approached by different parties who saw buying us as a big market play. Frankly, this freaked us out. After seventeen years doing our own thing with intense tunnel vision, we still had a kind of mom-and-pop attitude toward the business. We were reasonably smart and aggressive, but not in the same league as the investment bankers who kept knocking on our door. It was sort of like being the three little pigs up against a wolf with a whole lot of money.

After we turned down many opportunities, a competitor we knew well said he wanted to make a serious deal that could work out well for everybody. We'd been reading some of the books and articles about all the deals going on and thought it might be worth going through the drill as a learning experience. Smart business leaders meet with anybody who can teach them something. In this particular case, we found ourselves presented with an offer well below reality. I sat there politely while the bankers tried to justify the number with research on a market my brothers and I helped create.

Three years later, we got propositioned again by a company we had been working with very successfully as a strategic partner. Once again, I thought it might be valuable to see what the market was doing, and what they had in mind. Once again, the discussion ended quickly when it came to valuation. They were a very conservative team used to growing their business through acquisitions, and their rules of thumb were inflexible.

When the investment bankers tried to put a value on Beryl, they focused exclusively on standard factors like cash flow, EBITDA (Earnings Before Interest, Taxes, Depreciation, and Amortization), and technology infrastructure. In their world, where every business is a commodity like a chair or a pen, this approach is the only way of looking at things. I didn't want to hurt anybody's feelings by pointing out that culture and people were the assets that drove our growth. And I'm not talking about executive "talent." I'm talking about the real talent and the heart of the organization—the people who answer the phones.

WHAT GOES AROUND . . .

IF THERE IS A DEAL SOMEWHERE DOWN THE ROAD FOR US, I've decided that rather than look for it, I'm going to just let it come to me. More than likely it will just happen, like meeting my wife, and all the other milestones over the last twenty years did. It may be an issue my kids have to decide. After my discussions with the folks from the world of high finance, the enduring lesson I walked away with was how special a place Beryl is and how connected I've become to our family of coworkers. That is one relationship I don't have any desire to end.

When we hired Pat Benner, a chief financial officer who came from this intense world of high finance and who had a ton of merger and acquisition experience, it was interesting to see how much our culture blew his mind. He added a great deal of discipline we'd always lacked, but he was skeptical—to put it mildly—about all the dress-up days, talent contests, carnivals, book clubs, giveaways and practical jokes that flourish on the most superficial level of that culture.

In the end we won him over. He became not just a disciple, but a bit of a prophet as well. This happened in a flash of intuition one day en route to a meeting in Indiana after he and I had driven a half hour listening to the radio. All of a sudden he turned the volume down and said, "Your strategy is like a circle. Investing so much in our coworkers makes them extremely loyal and committed. When customers pick up on how focused our

people are, it drives client loyalty. That results in higher profit and we end up with more money to invest back in our coworkers. Then the circle of growth begins again."

I was flattered that this brilliant, analytical guy had finally signed off on the simple logic of our family-style approach, and we formally adopted his "**Circle of Growth**SM" metaphor as part of our corporate philosophy. His epiphany reinforced a hunch I've had ever since I got dissed by the coworker who liked to eat at Fat Burger.

The key to success for any business is people.

Period.

STAYING SMALL

MY BROTHERS AND I HAD GONE FROM sleeping on the cot in the little conference room to arguing with investment bankers about how much our business was worth. When you go from three people to three hundred, inevitably you have to ask yourself what the perfect size is for a business like yours. You end up wondering how the issue of size affects your daily operations and the value of the business.

When we were growing up, our father was probably our biggest role model. He steadily established a legal practice that gave us all a very nice life. Barry, Mark, and I also had two uncles we admired a great deal. One had a commercial linen supply and rental business. My other uncle had a food processing company where I worked a few summers driving a forklift when I was a kid. Like my dad, both my uncles built up businesses that enabled them to build security for their families. To this day, that's basically all I want out of life.

In 2006, Beryl had revenues of $25 million and 289 people on the payroll. I'm truly grateful that the example of my uncles inoculated me against the delusion that I need to be running a $250 million company, or that doing so would make me a better person or a more impressive human being. Personally, I've never felt the desire to have a public company or to be the CEO of a public company. It's so foreign to me that I can't imagine what it would be like. The only other real job I had before law school was working as a waiter.

During our acquisition negotiations, we did a lot of soul-searching. For the first time in my life I had to wonder what it would be like to run Beryl for somebody else. A buddy whose own firm had recently been bought out warned me point-blank: "It's a whole different world. As long as you're doing well, they'll leave you alone. But if you're not, they're on you."

This didn't sound promising. Ever since we dug our way out of debt, we'd enjoyed absolute control of our destiny. We got zero pressure to grow at a specific rate, and no investors held us accountable for anything. Growth had always exceeded our expectations anyway, probably because we'd always *acted* as if we had investors, a mentality every business owner should adopt. So why would our definition of success include being exposed to people who could push us in directions we didn't like? Why should we surrender control and suffer these uncertainties?

JUST FOR THE SAKE OF BEING BIG?

WE'D SEEN THE DISASTROUS RESULT of Wall Street's obsession with growth even in our own industry. Our main competitor, who was backed by venture capital funding, was under constant pressure to run his business a certain way. Because of this pressure, his "Circle of Growth" was spinning backwards—he was basically a slave to number-crunchers who forbade him from investing in his culture and his people. So he ended up with a lackluster workforce that couldn't hold on to his customer base. This forced him into the low-cost provider strategy and eventually into selling the business, which wouldn't have been his first choice.

By the time Beryl was perceived as a hot property, we'd been through a few crazy growth spurts of our own. After those experiences, again and again, we found ourselves instinctively turning down growth for growth's sake. We passed up a huge deal that would have doubled our size and we chose not to acquire half a dozen firms that looked like perfect strategic partners on paper. The more offers we got to expand, the more we were forced to ask ourselves fundamental questions about our company and the nature of business and management in general. Two years ago, the program we hammered out gained fame as a case study in Susan Annunzio's book *Contagious Success*, a business book about high-performing organizations.

JULIA'S STORY

March 15th is my last day here at Beryl, and I'm walking away with great stories to tell. First, I would like to tell you that the times spent working at Beryl have been the best years of my life. Not only with the people that have surrounded me through the years, but with all the people that I feel like I truly helped, including our customers.

There are many stories to tell, and I am going to walk away remembering the phone calls from callers who I felt like I helped—everyone from the first-time moms who signed up for childbirth classes to the dad who is trying to set up an appointment with a doctor but doesn't know what kind of doctor to choose. I felt in my heart that I assisted the callers in choosing everything from the right type of doctor to the right type of class. I felt like I have educated millions (sometimes it felt like millions!) of people on the difference between and MD and a DO to an HMO and a PPO. I've educated people on things as simple as what an ENT does to the difference between an internal medicine and a family practitioner. And when I went home, I felt the satisfaction that I really helped someone that day. Even now, when I am on the phone, I truly feel like the callers have called the right place because I believe in myself and in the fact that Beryl stands for connecting people to the right healthcare. I really believe that I made the right choice in working with Beryl all of these years because it brought me satisfaction. I could breathe a heavy sigh with a smile at the end of my day because I knew that I had done my best and I knew that I had helped.

We can hear the smiles when we are talking to customers over the phone; it's in the way they talk. You can hear the voice shaky at the onset of the call, but when we say, "Sure I can help you with that," you can hear them relax a little and by the time we conclude the call you can hear their voice change and you can hear them smile. Which makes me smile even bigger. Thank goodness that we're not robots or that we have what feels like a thousand different prompts to push before the caller gets to speak to someone who responds back. We give it that human touch; it's in the way we answer our calls and in the way we respond to the caller with genuine care.

There are a few stories that I'm going to walk away remembering for the rest of my life. When I had just started working at Beryl, there were only a few of us here, and a call came in. This man said he wanted to kill himself. I stayed on the phone with him for over an hour just listening to him and telling him I understood. All my coworkers were around me, patting me on the back, holding my hand, and smiling. That is what I'll never forget. Another time, a grandfather called from Mexico looking for his granddaughter who had been in a car accident. He knew she was in a New York hospital, but didn't know at which hospital. Even though we weren't supposed to call around to other hospitals, I did. I heard his voice, and I knew he needed the help. He thanked me over and over again and wanted to know where he could send me a gift. I told him that I didn't need one and that the fact that we found her was all the gift I needed. I felt really satisfied, and that feeling stayed with me for a long time. I just wanted to say that Beryl has that human touch. It's not only human, it's genuine.

Julia has been a Beryl coworker for over ten years.

CHAPTER TWO:

BUILDING A BRAND

V ery few companies, especially small ones, have famous brands like Coke® or Tide®. Do 1 percent of service providers have the name recognition of Federal Express or H & R Block? Not even half a percent do. The name Beryl is well-known today in the health-care industry, but it took my brothers and me twenty years to build a recognized brand. We learned firsthand how difficult the process can be, and we picked up a few practical lessons along the way.

Our first stab at branding was back in Los Angeles with Emergency Response Systems. We knew we had to develop some kind of aura around the company name. We wanted our industry to know that ERS had set the standard, and we wanted this standard to be something people would respect and something that all our coworkers lived by. Years later we'd learn that what we were calling an "aura" was more formally known as a brand promise.

When you're small and nobody knows who you are, you have no idea how to get on the path to market leadership. But in our own naïve way, we did develop a sort of mini-brand with ERS. It didn't take a genius to realize that building relationships through customer service is the single biggest opportunity for most businesses. This certainly always rang true for us. We were totally open to customer needs from the second we made contact, and it was largely interpersonal success with these individuals that earned ERS its reputation for outstanding service.

In the early days we had to drive all over Los Angeles to install our response units. Technically, the hospitals were our clients, but we spent the bulk of our personal time dealing with hospital patients in their homes. Whichever two brothers weren't watching the monitor would pile the tools into a car and drive out to connect the new patient to the system. One Friday afternoon it took Mark and me four and a half hours to get through traffic and find an address. When we finally got there the woman asked us if we'd mind getting back on the highway to pick her up some Häagen Dazs.

By then, it was now six o'clock, and the city's notorious gridlock was frozen solid. It had been a long week, and frankly, running errands like this had never crossed my mind when I was putting the business plan together. But we did what every smart entrepreneur has to do. We smiled and said, "What flavor?" An hour later, when we got back with this patient's pint of butter pecan, I counted out the change on the kitchen table. When I gave her the receipt, she gave me a smile that told me we had won her over completely.

I doubt this senior citizen sent us out to fetch ice cream as some kind of test, but that's not the point. The point is that when we ran her errand and acted as if she had every right to ask us, she knew we were the kind of people that she could trust with her personal security. She could tell right away that if she ever had problems with the equipment, we'd come back out, fix it, and not leave her exposed to the danger of her medical condition. Like many other patients we treated the same way, she let our hospital client know how impressed she was with ERS.

That lesson on the importance of trust is basically what made The Beryl Companies. We owe every contract we've ever won to the same idealistic spirit of service. I detail specific service tactics in the following chapter, but from a branding viewpoint, the important thing is to make sure your customers know you will go to any end for them, regardless of circumstances. And you will do so, if not with genuine enthusiasm, then at least with civility, understanding, and dependability.

The pint of butter pecan ice cream is another important symbol for me, because I have sat through several long discussions with people who seem to view branding as an abstract science. From years of personal experience, I know that it's simply the little things we consistently do for people that make the Beryl name and that continue to enhance and solidify the brand. Idealism has its rewards, and any company that develops a real passion for these small service details will benefit in a number of ways. A reputation for stellar service is a sure path to the premium-provider status that guarantees leverage in pricing.

THE "STORY" OF OUR NAME

WHEN WE PURCHASED OUR TEXAS CALL CENTER IN 1998, it was time to change the name of the company to reflect the fact that we were doing different things. Anybody who has gone through one of these naming exercises knows how important names are to the corporate image. There's always a desire for the perfect marriage between the words and the reality of what the company does.

During this period, Mark was taking flying lessons at a flight school in Santa Monica. The receptionist was a very pretty girl from Italy who liked to wear jewelry with lots of unusual gemstones. Thinking he might want to ask her out, Mark bought a book on gemstones to learn a little bit about this interest of hers. Flipping through the book, he came across the section on beryl and it caught his imagination.

Beryl is a family of gemstones that come in an unusual variety of colors, from rose to gold to emerald green. He showed Barry and me, and we all thought the name was a great symbol for a unique family business where each of the owners had different talents and all the coworkers were very distinct individuals. That was it! The receptionist moved back to Italy, but we got a distinctive and versatile name that has helped us articulate our culture and brand.

We've built a whole corporate "story" around the name. Internally, we tapped into the jewelry theme by dividing customers into "platinum," "gold," and "silver" categories. We promote our service platform as "Emerald Care^SM." A driving metaphor that has been easy for coworkers to grasp is our goal of delivering service "gems" to every customer. A "gem" can be anything from a tangible present like a gift basket to a really outstanding interaction over the phone by a call advisor. Gem stands for Great Employee Moments. Going to get the Häagen Dazs twenty years ago was probably our first service gem.

It's still a priority for me to try to deliver as many personal gems as I can. As CEO, it's not necessary for me to get on a plane and fly out to sit down with the marketing directors of small hospitals. I don't need to spend an hour or two asking those customers detailed questions about how well the account executives are taking care of them. I know our people smother them with attention. But when I get up to shake hands after a visit like this, I usually get the old butter pecan smile. If this sounds like a corny feel-good crusade, I know for a fact that my making it a point to touch these smaller customers is one reason why our client retention rate holds steady.

When was the last time you delivered a "gem" to a client? How often do you lose the ones you can't make time to do something small for?

THE NEED FOR A "BIG" IMPRESSION

SINCE WE FORMALLY BECAME THE BERYL COMPANIES eight years ago, I have given my card to bankers, journalists, graduate school professors, and a lot of fellow CEOs. In that entire time, only one person, a young man who works in our mailroom, has ever asked me how many "companies" Beryl actually runs. The answer is one. Back in 1998, we didn't have multiple companies, but thought that some day we might. Being practical people, we didn't want to redo expensive collateral materials when we diversified.

Honestly, we probably wanted to sound bigger than we really were. From the day we opened our doors, we were always preoccupied with the impression we made on clients. Here's a silly example that some business owners might be able to relate to. In the first proper office we leased in Los Angeles, we built ten cubicles for call advisors. At the time, we only needed two because we only had a few clients. When prospects were scheduled to tour this facility, we'd round up friends in other offices down the hall. They'd come over for a few minutes, put on headsets, and pretend to be Beryl workers answering calls.

We were young men determined to grow our business, and we knew that certain clients simply would not sign on with a tiny start-up. To us, faking a few call advisors was not a devious deception. We knew we could staff up to handle any contract we were bidding, and we serviced every contract we won exceptionally well. Looking back from where Beryl is today, from a mature ethical viewpoint where honesty outranks every other value, I'm not especially proud of that trick.

But our bogus advisor episode is a good illustration of the obsession every ambitious business has with client perceptions. And ten years later, when we branded our single company as a set of "companies," we probably still thought that the size and scope of our operation were the most important measures of how good we were at what we did. We were angling for a bigger class of client then, and we assumed these prospects would be more comfortable with a provider that sounded like a hefty corporate entity. It was about the same time that we began to use public relations in a strategic fashion to help us magnify the impressions we made on prospective clients and the industry in general.

Strategic PR turned out to be the honest way of achieving the impressive effects we'd handled so immaturely in the past.

HOW PUBLIC RELATIONS HELPED US

MANY EXECS ARE HESITANT TO SPEND A LOT OF MONEY on public relations, but next to phenomenal customer service, we've found that it is the best way to grow a business. Working smart PR campaigns persistently and cycling the right messages to our different audiences have seriously strengthened our brand. We continue to benefit from a full range of techniques, and I've been stunned by the potential of something as basic as a press release. We had to start with these basics because there is nothing inherently sexy about what we do. Beryl has never been any PR firm's idea of a dream client.

FULL-COURT PRESS

WE STARTED SENDING RELEASES TO THE PRESS about every contract we signed and direct-mailing copies to every client and potential customer we could identify—to anybody we wanted to know about Beryl. It took a while to flesh out a really comprehensive list of business contacts, but six months into this direct mail campaign, I started getting lots of feedback: "You guys are really growing!" "Wow, Beryl is going gangbusters!"

This wasn't really the case. In most of the releases, we were just adding another client and maybe a few extra thousand dollars a month to our revenue. But the cumulative effect of all the announcements gave a much different impression. After we'd run the campaign for two years, our sales director called on a very prestigious account for the first time and found out that our reputation preceded her. She asked, "How did you hear about Beryl?" The prospect said, "How can you be in New York and *not* know about Beryl?" It was such a huge compliment for us in that particular market that when I heard the story, I knew the PR was really clicking. Worked patiently, this single tactic created a reputation for us to the point where if you're in healthcare today, looking at the kinds of services we provide, you know who Beryl is.

Before we achieved this level of name recognition, I was always concerned that there might be a big contract up for bid someplace in the country that we didn't know anything about. Our PR efforts put that concern to bed and kept us from missing out on several significant competitions. By the time prospects had thrown twenty or thirty of our mailers in the trash, they had put one of them in a vendor file. And they'd gotten the message that we were the best at what we did. We still list our biggest accounts on releases so prospects have always known that we're the partner of choice for a lot of important hospitals. This helped us win a lot of bids.

When we saw how well the press releases worked, we sat down with our agency and started looking for other platforms and messages that would keep bolstering the positive impression. This quest sparked a dynamic internal marketing debate that sharpened our understanding of our mission. It was a PR brainstorming session, in fact, that helped us realize that nobody else in our industry had access to all the different kinds of data Beryl did. This realization would eventually transform our entire business.

MARKET INTELLIGENCE . . . FREE!

OUR CALL ADVISORS HAVE SERVICED THE FRONTLINE marketing campaigns for hundreds of hospitals all over the United States, from small community facilities to world-famous teaching universities. On any given day, we know which aspects of these campaigns are clicking with different consumer markets and which ones are falling flat. These are precisely the things that every marketing director in the healthcare industry lies awake at night worrying about. What is my competitor doing? How do I measure up? Which way do we go next year? How can I promote programs that really drive business?

It's helpful to keep in mind that until recently, healthcare has not traditionally been the most innovative marketing environment in the world. Selling an MRI appointment is not like selling an iPOD. Your creative options are restricted, and when a good idea finally does come along, people want to know about it and take advantage of it.

So as a new wrinkle in our message cycle, I started sending every client an e-mail we called the "Beryl Weekly Update." The format was something I'd seen an old client use very effectively with his coworkers. We evolved it into a slick, short newsletter full of the best practices and hard intelligence on our market.

At times, the weekly update has seemed like one of those brilliant ideas you wish you never had. Each punchy little text takes a surprising amount of work to put together, and suggestions have been made that we cut back to biweekly or once a month. But I haven't missed a week for years and hope I never will. I don't care if I'm on vacation. Wherever I am, I make sure the weekly update goes out.

The discipline has paid off in many ways. The weekly update generates sales, but that's not why we keep going through the hassle. In the final analysis, the update is strategic ice cream—something extra we do for people who do business with us, a little freebie PR favor that proves our commitment to service. And it definitely makes clients smile. For many, the update has become an important part of their planning and budgeting efforts. The fact is, they can't get the information anywhere else. Why not flaunt a signature capability that sets Beryl apart?

Almost every business that's really engaged in its industry can offer clients some sort of valuable advice or market intelligence on a regular basis. If you had to send your clients a best practice update today, what would you tell them? If you went through the exercise of putting together twelve monthly updates, would you know your own market better? Would those perspectives help you with your own planning?

As soon as we started making sales off the weekly updates, we sat down with our agency to figure out how else we could use our information resources to build up the brand. In 2002, we worked some client case studies and basic trend analyses into whitepapers that led us to publish our first *National Benchmarking Study* two years later.

The benchmarking study was essentially a compilation of data that let our clients gauge how well they were doing in terms of the caller experience.

The positive exposure we got from the study was tremendous. For the first time in our industry, a community hospital in a major metropolitan market could use this report to measure its performance against similar institutions. Were they getting the same results for their campaign in terms of call volume? Did they have a proper ratio of male and female callers? Was the Internet impacting them any differently than the norm? Once again, by a significant margin, we proved that Beryl is the only source for a lot of this information.

THE BERYL INSTITUTE

WE DRILLED THAT MESSAGE HOME IN 2006 when we founded The Beryl Institute. The institute is a thought-based leadership platform that positions our company as the true experts in healthcare customer service and customer interaction. The formal mission is to raise the overall level of customer service in an industry not known for valuing the customer's experience. We do this, and have enhanced our brand significantly, through educational speaking engagements and the publication of timely studies. Even as a relatively small company, we were increasingly viewed as the market authority and as a premium provider with a uniquely altruistic set of values. It is true that all PR is good, and our intensive customer service culture has genuinely evolved a public service element.

Establishing ourselves as a thought leader helped our performance as well as our reputation, because The Beryl Institute has been a great motivator for our coworkers. The messaging helps them realize that by "connecting people to healthcare" they actually do serve a higher purpose in society. PR that boosts morale across an organization is invaluable. Ultimately your people *are* your brand, and they apply themselves a lot more enthusiastically when they feel their efforts make a difference.

YOUR BRAND IS ALIVE

COWORKERS AS BRAND ASSETS is another obvious reality that seems to get overlooked a lot. I'm amazed by how many small businesses I encounter with perfect concepts, brilliant imagery, and people on the payroll who are dropping balls left, right, and center. The owners obviously agonized over their logos and the look and feel of their collateral. And I can understand that. I've always felt that the quality of our brochures, presentations, and proposals was as important as what we had to say. I like custom photography and outsized formats and never skimp on creative or production dollars.

But once you dazzle your prospects, you have to hand them over to your people. Every one of them needs to embody the brand at least as well as the fancy brochure.

Beryl's long-time sales star Linda Cota-Robles flawlessly exemplifies our professionalism and standards of quality. Originally working as a competitor, Linda just celebrated her nineteenth anniversary with the company. During the nearly-two decades that she has represented Beryl in our most critical public forums, I cannot remember her ever dropping a ball. Clients can't, either: they all see a refined, soft-selling person who always does precisely what she says she's going to do. Much of our success today is directly due to Linda and the innumerable positive impressions she has made.

It goes without saying that our bread and butter and chief claim to fame are the very human voices and unique personalities of hundreds of call advisors. To the outside world, these people are Beryl. That's why we put them on top of the organization chart. Even coworkers who don't interface directly with external audiences have a huge impact on how the company is perceived. The main focus of our culture programs is to make sure that every coworker adds power to the company's public image. We try to inspire real passion in our people and share it with the world outside.

CLIENT TESTIMONIALS

IN MY OPINION, MOST COMPANIES UNDERUTILIZE their clients as a branding resource. Beryl brings these outside assets inside the family, forming extremely loyal relationships that play out on many different levels. Initiatives like our annual client conference help develop this community. The conference is a national three-day event we've held in October for the past five years. We bring all of our customers to Dallas so they can get together and dialogue. We're careful to keep Beryl as only a small part of the formal agenda, but the clients invariably end up talking about what it's like to work with us.

We bring in speakers to facilitate the conversation. To keep the spotlight on clients and their concerns, we have a "marketing gallery," where they can showcase their own programs and see what their peers are up to. The event is a very productive networking and education session that feels like a vacation for these busy folks. It's more PR ice cream that contributes mightily to our retention rate.

Because our relationships with many key clients have grown into genuine friendships, we don't hesitate to use them as references. When we pitch to new business possibilities, we encourage every prospect to talk to people who have used us. We say,

"Don't believe us. Call Marianne Coughlin at The Mount Sinai Medical Center. Or Pedro Ibarbia at New York Presbyterian Hospital. Call Ann Marie Bonvini at Yale New Haven Health." Some of these client-friends may get thirty calls a year from our prospects. They're happy to take them, and their testimonials make all the difference in the world.

RAISING THE BAR: THE EXECUTIVE ADVISORY COUNCIL

ANOTHER GROUP OF OUTSIDERS who helped burnish our image is our Executive Advisory Council. This group came into being fairly recently when we decided to expand the scope of our services.

Our new goal is to touch individual healthcare consumers throughout their entire continuum of care. To do this, Beryl is moving beyond marketing into the much larger world of healthcare operations. Our call advisors will perform all kinds of new services: things like making outbound calls to confirm appointments and conducting post discharge phone calls. It's a logical evolution that will improve the average American patient's overall healthcare experience. Having set the standard years ago, we want to raise the bar.

In the somewhat bureaucratic world of hospital management, however, we realized that we faced a big challenge. We knew virtually every hospital marketing director in our target market, but very few chief medical officers, chief financial officers, or chief operating officers. Our company wasn't even on their radar screens. So we had to ask ourselves: "How do we get to the table in the c-suite?"

The answer was that we needed help opening doors.

Alan Weinstein is a successful healthcare veteran, a friend, and a great consultant who is extremely well-connected. He knew what we wanted to do and approached me with the concept of putting together a group of primarily retired hospital or healthcare CEOs. These people could help us focus our strategy and propel the business forward. The new Executive Advisory Council wasn't going to be a board of directors. They were there to help build relationships. The reason we purposely sought out mostly retired execs was to avoid conflicts of interest.

From the first meeting this group far exceeded every expectation. We assembled such a "who's who" in healthcare that it's been humbling to think that men and women of this caliber would agree to help a small company develop its messages. They are all deeply experienced managers who are still passionate about what they're doing and are very open and honest with us about our core business.

A SCANDAL WE COULD HANDLE

OUR ASSOCIATION WITH THE COUNCIL put us in a whole new league in terms of how the company was perceived. But our public debut was rocky! The premier trade publication in our industry is *Modern Healthcare*. We had never been able to score a mention in this excellent magazine before, but as soon as we sent out a press release about the council, we got a callback from a reporter who wanted to do a big story.

The interview was upbeat and left me thinking the article was going to be totally positive. I was really pumped—until the issue came out!

One of our council members at the time happened to chair an industry regulatory board. This particular individual has such a golden reputation that it never crossed anybody's mind that he could be accused of doing anything dicey. It certainly never crossed my mind, or his, or Alan Weinstein's, or any of the super-sharp minds on the council.

The reporter, on the other hand, thought an unsubstantiated whiff of scandal made for good reading. So, after two decades of polishing the Beryl brand until it truly did shine like a gemstone, I found myself sitting in my office one morning reading a big story in the industry bible that didn't necessarily put us in a positive light.

Fortunately, events proved that perception is a two-way street. In the next issue of the magazine, one of the most prominent healthcare attorneys in the country wrote an outraged letter to the editor. He rebutted the article point by point and said that if seasoned mentors couldn't help well-meaning smaller companies improve their business, the ultimate loser would be the average American consumer. This argument carried the day, thank goodness. The next time the magazine mentioned the council, the coverage made it clear that what Beryl was doing was not only legitimate, but innovative and noteworthy.

As time passed, the council helped dramatically improve our dialogue with the publication, which, for years, had published a prestigious list of the top outsourcing companies in healthcare. Beryl had been excluded from consideration because the magazine's criteria insisted the outsourcing firms must operate on-site in the healthcare facilities. Through the liaison work of a council member who knew people at the magazine, I was actually able to propose a modified definition that included off-site firms. As a result, Beryl was ranked ninth on the next list.

Throughout our tense little media flap, I was advised that if a company is working its PR cycle aggressively, one or two messages are bound to get butchered. So if you ever find yourself confronted with a similar splash of "bad ink," try to remember that while the blood is draining from your face in horror, it is all part of building the brand, a chore you can't ignore.

KEEPING YOUR SHINE

THE LONGER YOU'VE BEEN IN THE PUBLIC EYE, the more pressure there is to keep up the mystique. It's one of the challenges I enjoy most, particularly when the messages have to do with customer service. A leader has to stay intimately involved in determining how his or her customers are treated. Senior management is ultimately responsible for the delivery of the brand promise, but I bombard my team with ideas all the time. They're not all good ideas, but I throw them out just the same.

The risk of losing market dominance is what keeps me awake at night. You can shrug off a fluke story in a magazine, but a slump in customer service standards can cost you everything you've worked so hard to build. Your bright and shining brand is guaranteed to lose luster the minute it ceases to be a top prior-ity in-house. That's why I make sure *everybody* understands the importance of this issue.

Like 99.5 percent of businesses, Beryl does not have an inherently breathtaking story to tell. We're the best at what we do, and what we do is socially important, but it's not front-page news. Yet my experience with the basic outreach function of PR has sold me forever on the discipline. Technically, when we sent out our first press release, we could probably still be called a call center company. We were perceived as a commodity business that competed on price and had no right to charge a premium for its services. By the time we rolled out The Beryl Institute, we were looked at by customers as a premium provider and by the financial market as an information business with a markedly higher valuation than our competitors.

Any small business owner can use PR as a force multiplier if you work your message cycle creatively and relentlessly. Don't forget that PR strategy requires a leader's time and attention. Once we'd evolved our cycle, we were telling our story with a lot more confidence and conviction. In a modern market where "small" is no longer a stigma, we stopped wasting time trying to act big, look big, and sound big. We'd learned that what truly made us different was the intensity of our commitment to service and the culture programs that drive our service ethic.

Now that we were the premium provider in our industry, it didn't make any difference what size we were.

JOHN'S STORY

I used to work at EDS right after GM bought the company and Ross Perot was walking around describing himself as "the sand in the oyster." What he was trying to say was that if he had to be an irritant to generate some valuable results for the corporation, so be it. I think I've developed a reputation as the sand in the oyster here at Beryl.

Three or four years ago, when we won our first "Best Place to Work" award, everybody in the company but me was walking around wearing a "Best Place to Work" T-shirt. People kept coming up to me and saying, "Where's your T-shirt?"

I said, "I'm not wearing it. Right now, personally, I don't consider this the best place to work."

Everybody thought I was going to get fired, and I finally got so annoyed I went up to Paul and said, "You know what? I'm not the only person around here who thinks this isn't the best place to work. I just want to tell you how it is."

He got very concerned and said, "What do you mean?" So I ran through some issues with him, most of which touched on communication between departments.

It wasn't too long after that conversation that he kicked off the Texas Christian University study. A huge SWAT team of MBAs came in and talked to everybody to try to figure out what was wrong with communications at Beryl.

It's still not Utopia here, but no workplace is ever going to be perfect. I get a lot of freedom to do what I want with technology. It's essentially an open campus. I'm usually happy because you're always proving yourself and I appreciate the luxury of being able to do a lot of different things. In my opinion, our data potential is really what makes us special. It's so valuable it will be interesting to see how we mature the asset.

I think we go a little overboard sometimes trying to make everybody happy, and I continue to speak my mind. When you start believing your own press releases, that's when your competitors pass you by. But at least Paul is approachable. You can talk to the guy.

John is the company's LAN and data security manager.

CHAPTER THREE:

BECOMING A PREMIUM PROVIDER

W hat does it mean to be a premium provider? To me it means not being a low-cost provider or a commodity business. If the firm you own or manage basically competes on price, how can you break out of that trap? How can you evolve your operation into a non-commodity business that generates solid profits? At Beryl, we've spent the last twenty years doing just that. It's an ongoing battle, believe me.

Many people who don't know the company well would still look at us and say, "Oh, you're in the call center business!" As soon as they learn that we have people answering phones, they assume that we run a telemarketing boiler room. They assume our call advisors are untrained job-jumpers who peddle junk all day. To become a premium provider, we had to overcome those misperceptions and develop a more sophisticated business that generated higher returns than the high volume sweatshops.

The decision was an easy one. We couldn't afford to be looked at as a commodity business. With rare exceptions, the biggest public call center companies have low market valuations and thin margins. As with any other company, my brothers and I wanted to build long-term value and operate with maximized margins. Long before we found our niche as an information company, we broke Beryl out of the call center mold by determining not to be a low-cost competitor.

CHOOSE TO SET THE PRICE

BERYL DOESN'T COMPETE DIRECTLY with these big public companies in our healthcare niche, but we do measure ourselves against them in terms of profitability. Only one has consistently matched our profit margin range.

The beauty of upgrading our call center model from a commodity business is that when you do this correctly, the scale upsides increase significantly. Pricing at a premium, we can still maximize scale in the operation and drive efficiencies by using call advisors to answer phones for multiple institutions and healthcare organizations. These efficiencies combined with the more aggressive pricing strategy to give us escalating profit margins year over year.

For a small company, it usually takes a while to figure out reasonable models, what your costs are, and how to be profitable. To price for profit, you have to make sure your customers feel like they are receiving value beyond the current commodity price. With careful positioning, extraordinary service, and a progressive, people-oriented culture, most commodity businesses can evolve into the premium provider model. All these things will help you sell at a premium and prove that you're worth it.

PRICING DISCIPLINE: BE WILLING TO LOSE

BERYL ISN'T FOR EVERYBODY. There are a lot of choices when you buy a car, a lot of choices when you go out to dinner, and lots of customer interaction companies. In the same way every potential coworker is not a fit for us, we're not a fit for every potential customer. We are very proud of the fact that we deliver the best quality in the market. We are very up-front and open about the fact that a client must be willing to pay for this quality. If he or she decides to go with a provider who offers a different level of service at a lower cost, by all means, we respect that. Here's a supportive e-mail a coworker sent me:

Gary F. (5/6/05)
Subject: Monthly CEO Letter

Paul:

Every company for which I have worked in the past has talked about being committed to quality. But when it got right down to brass tacks, they always, without exception, sacrificed quality to save a few dollars, or increase their bonuses, or shorten their schedules, etc. I have yet to find that the case here and I am thankful. I understand the importance of these dynamics but I also understand the costs of cutting back on quality. You seem to have found a good balance. Thank you for your commitment to quality.

He's seen us walk away from very attractive pieces of business rather than sacrifice our performance standards and the pricing structure they support. And it's never easy to walk away from any piece of business. Over the years, there have been a number of situations where I'd wished I could drop our price because it might have been nice to work with a particular organization. In hindsight, sticking to our guns has allowed us to work with people who want to work with us. They realize our value because they share our values. It's quite unlikely that prospects who don't share our values will end up as long-term customers anyway. They'll never get completely engaged in what we're trying to do for them, so they won't understand the full importance of the service. A year from now, or two years from now, when a competitor comes in and says he can do it cheaper, they're going to listen, and they might leave. We want and get loyal customers who don't shop.

We'd rather be choosy and walk away from those that we can't sell on the value. We know that we've built enough of a brand and enough of a reputation so that, more often than not, people are willing to make Beryl their choice. The results are evident in how successful we are against competition and in our long-term relationships. In our lobby, we have flat screens that cycle through our client roster, and we're proud to display many clients we've held onto for more than a decade.

You always have to balance efficiency and quality against your pricing and profits. If you only drive toward profit, quality will suffer. Just set your own price bar and try to balance your service standards against it. And remember: if you can't deliver profit, you won't be able to invest in technology or expand the lives of the people who work for you. Do your low-cost competitors make money? Ours don't. They can't cut it in the long run and end up going out of business or being forced to sell.

That's not to say the landscape won't change. We're not so arrogant as to think we can ratchet up rates and people will pay anything for what we do. Business doesn't work like that. You have to deliver value. It's a growing market and new competitors will keep appearing, but our service reputation gives us a major head start as long as we continue to deliver. We're certainly not afraid of competitors approaching our customers. Premium providers have loyal customer bases. The beauty of that is being able to leverage your credibility and go back to sell these clients again and again. If we have to react to market swings, it won't be by lowering our prices or standards.

QUANTIFY YOUR VALUE

WE DIDN'T FULLY REALIZE THE TRUE DETAILED cost of our service until 1999 and 2000. Before that, in a lot of situations, we were the only company our clients were looking at. We knew that wouldn't last forever, but once competitors did come flocking into our niche, we were surprised to hear they were charging so much less. Management in healthcare marketing is always challenging every dollar, so when vendors promise they can save money, the client is going to listen. In certain bid situations, our costs looked 40 percent higher! It was a threat and we knew we had to react. We could either cut our prices or quantify the value Beryl delivers.

The first thing we had to do was to educate current and prospective clients about the pricing itself. Our competitors don't necessarily price the same way we do or use the same method. So our first step was to say, "Here, let us help you do an apples to apples comparison." We took time to make sure people understood that we charge by the minute, while company B charges by the call, and company C doesn't bother to include phone charges in its quotes. With this context for reference, bid reviewers could see that in many cases, our competitors weren't really much cheaper.

It was during this pricing reeducation campaign that we first noticed some clients weren't completely engaged in what we do for them. Some thought that all we did was answer phones. So we very carefully sat every client down and reeducated them about how we compare to our competitors in terms of service. We started by looking at the most basic services. How well do our advisors actually pick up and answer the phones? Do we do that on time and with a high level of customer service? We made sure clients understood that even though answering phones is just a small part of what we do, we execute that function a whole lot better than everybody else, and not just in terms of picking up quickly.

Most of our clients already knew that our advisors handled their customers' calls with a much higher level of compassion and patience than is required in a typical customer service situation. They knew our advisors were dealing with human problems and with callers who were either sick or trying to assist sick family members or loved ones. They understood that we had a complex infrastructure in place to ensure that every caller's need was met with empathy. What we learned that we had never properly explained before was the long-term financial impact of all this and the incremental patient revenues that Beryl's service quality generated for our clients. Once we were able to do this, we reestablished ourselves in their eyes not only as an innovative information and referral source, but as an indispensable partner.

COMPETITIVE POSITIONING

TO BREAK OURSELVES OUT OF THE PACK, we had to quantify the value we provided beyond the calls themselves. We had to explain that Beryl's real value isn't just world-class customer service. It's the power of the data we give back to the client. We proved to the hospital marketing directors that this data can help them grow their business and improve their job security. We taught them how to brief their CEOs and CFOs on the way this data enables sophisticated marketing campaigns that generate higher profits for the hospital. In other words, we demonstrated our value in ways the customer cared about.

As our reeducation program developed, we got increasingly better at convincing these marketing directors that Beryl's continuing participation was their best chance for career success and for an increased marketing budget. We loved making this final argument, because when marketing budgets rise, the phone rings more and Beryl makes more money! We closed the reeducation loop by showing our clients how to turn our information into powerful databases they could use to build on customer interactions. Customer Relationship Management (CRM) is something very new to healthcare and something most of these organizations don't do very well yet.

Positioning ourselves as an information company with expertise in CRM and ROI measurement really helped us defend ourselves against the new flock of low-cost competitors. The more we coached clients on how to use the customer knowledge our advisors capture for them, the more closely we bonded with these marketing vice presidents. We taught them how to use simple demographics, things like birthdates, and whether or not their callers have children, to predict with a high level of accuracy what level of healthcare services those callers will need in the future. As hospitals compete for a shrinking healthcare dollar and really focus on service for the first time in history, this data becomes invaluable in terms of building long-term relationships with their patients.

For added credibility, we commissioned a third party to do an independent "mystery shopper" study between Beryl and our two largest competitors, comparing our respective levels of service for our customers. We delivered the results to every current customer, whether they had been approached by competitors or not. The differences were compelling. We objectively proved that the satisfaction of working with Beryl, strictly from the call management side, was at a much higher level than with any other firm. This made us feel good and immediately helped us retain some of our business that might have left. Some of our least engaged clients weren't completely convinced of the Beryl difference until we actually put this third party validation in their hands.

In the modern business world, it's very easy to make an argument for the power of data. Another argument that smart small business owners should try to strengthen is the power of their cultures. We schooled clients on the human angle every bit as intensively as the technology factor. I can remember a specific instance where a large client was enamored by a competitor who wowed them with what seemed to be great new technology and a promise for service at a lower cost. We convinced them that while technology certainly drives our processes, we are fundamentally in the people business. Once they understood that happy Beryl call advisors significantly bump the satisfaction and loyalty of their callers and patients, they were happy to pay more. The average client will have a steeper learning curve as you try to educate him or her on the value of a progressive culture, but once they finally get it, price will no longer be an issue. They'll realize the upside of contracting with an innovative, dynamic firm where morale is sky-high and super-low turnover rates offer the invaluable guarantee of consistent, high-quality service. The basics of our culture program are outlined in the next chapter.

Proper positioning as a premium provider wasn't something we could accomplish over night. It took time and patience, but it's made all the difference in the world.

SELL LIKE A PREMIUM PROVIDER

CONVINCING A CLIENT THAT YOUR COMPANY is a premium provider starts with how you sell. We've established a reputation for responding immediately to prospects and handling them meticulously throughout the sales cycle. I'm shocked at the number of people who tell me that Beryl set itself apart simply by doing what we said we were going to do and delivering things on the day we promised to deliver them. I assumed all companies do that, but apparently, it isn't so. Knowing we kept our promises in the sales process gave these prospects confidence that we would keep our promises when it came time to execute on the relationship.

An experience with a prospect for our nurse telephone triage services proves this. We were fairly new to this line of business at the time, competing against a low-cost provider with a lot more experience. Technically, they had a much better shot at a deal that we won largely on finesse. When the primary contact came to tour our site, we picked her up at the airport and took her to dinner. When she got to her hotel room, there was a gorgeous wrapped basket of goodies waiting and a personal note card from me welcoming her to Dallas. None of this had anything to do with the service we were going to provide. We still had to prove we had the capability to deliver that. But we made it easy for her to see how she'd be treated as a customer.

Once she fell in love with Beryl, she told us how our competitor handled his site tour. Nobody picked her up at the airport; nobody even offered. So she called the salesperson, who was home in bed, and asked him, "Now what should I do?" He gave her the names of a few hotels and said, "You might want to call these." He lost the sale when he told her to take a cab to meet him at his company in the morning. But her sales horror story continued. When she finally got to the headquarters, nobody was prepped on her visit. Nobody important had time to meet her. Nobody was even aware that a potential customer was in the building.

After we close a deal, I always ask the customer why he or she chose Beryl. Before I started doing this, I would have assumed everybody would say it was because they thought we were going to provide better service than the competitor. The answer is almost always "the salesperson." It's always about people. Credibility and reputation in the marketplace are big factors, but it is astounding how much impact the human element has in the courtship phase. Even if your brand shines blazing bright, nothing promises premium-quality service better than premium-quality selling.

DETAILS AND THE PERSONAL TOUCH

EVERY HUMAN BEING HAS LOTS OF STORIES about good customer experiences and truly horrible ones. I constantly bring mine back to our senior management group and encourage them to share theirs. Recently I sent multiple messages back from a hotel in California with one of the best service philosophies I've ever seen. This particular hotel management team has the same obsession with details that I do. When they brought the crib for my infant son, there was a neat little kit with miniature wipes, baby powder, and lotions. It probably cost five bucks, but it made a huge impression on my wife and me. It's little things like this that keep us coming back year after year.

When we arrived at this hotel, the general manager had a nice gift basket with a personal note in the room welcoming us back. But that's not enough for this premium sales maestro. He knows that, in the final analysis, customer service is just a tenacious continuation of the sales cycle. That's why he never lets up. When we came back to our room the second night there was a fancier cheese and fruit plate, another bottle of wine and a second well-composed personal note that went on very convincingly about how much my business meant to the hotel and to him personally.

This beautifully orchestrated treatment gave me a severe case of customer service envy. I immediately started wondering what Beryl does for *our* visiting prospects and clients the second night they come back to their rooms. As a result, when clients visit us today, we put strawberries and chocolates in their rooms on the second night so they'll have something nice to munch on before they go to sleep.

Real premium providers are passionate about these indispensable caring gestures and the personal touch. When guests visit our facility, we serve branded Beryl water. It has its own label, looks great and costs less in bulk than water at the store. I stole the idea from a car dealership.

When we sign on new clients, they get a "welcome wagon." This little Flexible Flyer stuffed with goodies is our way of saying, "Welcome to the family." I get so many calls from people who think it's just the neatest thing. What did it cost us? Thirty dollars? For a relationship that could mean hundreds of thousands of dollars, even millions over the course of time, it's insane not to do things like this.

You are not "premium selling" if you don't recognize the life events of your customers. When we meet prospects we want to know their birthday, their wedding anniversary and what hobbies they have. One of our clients collects elephant figurines. How difficult is it for us throughout the year to keep an eye open for unusual elephant carvings and to bring them to him on calls or send him another one for the holidays?

Pretend for a second that your real passion in life is elephant statuettes. If you knew that every time you saw the Beryl account executive you were going to get a cool new elephant to add to your collection, wouldn't you value that company over another outfit whose sales reps just want a commission? Sales and customer service relationships are all about *knowing people*.

Mistakes are details that premium providers take very seriously. *Nobody* does everything right all the time, and we're not perfect, either. Sometimes we get customers who are upset with us over a task that a coworker may have executed incorrectly. Our ingrained obsession with service helps us turn these slips around in a way that leaves an overall positive impression. What customers tend to remember is how quickly and sincerely we react. Because when something goes wrong, we're open and honest about it, and we jump all over it. We apologize and fix the problem immediately. That's the only kind of response that reinforces credibility and a sense of partnership.

TEACHING PREMIUM SERVICE

NOBODY STARTS WORKING FOR US until they've been carefully screened to make sure they have the potential to deliver the kind of service we can price at a premium. To activate that potential, we put every new hire though "Emerald Care" and "Best Foot Forward," training programs on how to treat callers, visitors, coworkers, and anybody else they encounter while representing The Beryl Companies. The program keeps the customer service focus intense and consistent across the organization.

Emerald Care is so successful, a number of clients have asked us to train their customer service people. For example, we had a client in New York that was getting lots of compliments on the way we handled their physician referral business and lots of complaints about the way calls were being handled by their schedulers and other touch points within the facility. Lara Fields, who leads our human resources group, flew out to brief her peers on the client side about specific recruiting, training and culture development techniques. In spite of the fact that we're not in the business of revamping our client's cultures, she gets quite a few similar requests for informal advice and we gladly respond to every one.

Our authority as a teacher of premium service raises our value in clients' eyes astronomically. It gives them another chance to think, "Wow, these people aren't just answering our phones—they're *making us better*." There is no higher compliment to a customer service company than clients begging to learn your premium-service secrets. Since the next client tends to come from the last client, this reputation for mentoring has also been good for new business.

Once again, when it came to developing the Emerald Care curriculum and training in a consistent way, we simply had no choice. Our sales people are out there making promises to prospects about a premium-priced service that is measurably superior in action. To deliver on those commitments consistently, we have to document our customer service techniques, train on these tactics, and make sure everybody is clear on the overall philosophy.

Training our people in customer service creates consistency, and I am a consistency freak. At Beryl, I'm trying to build the kind of environment that produces satisfaction in every customer experience. I want to be able to tell clients that they can safely bet their business on this environment because, really, that's what they're doing.

AVOIDING OFFSHORING

OVER THE LAST FEW YEARS, we've all seen how outsourcing and globalization have resulted in a tremendous amount of offshoring. The prime business functions sent overseas are IT infrastructure and customer service or call center work. Whether it's India, the Philippines, Jamaica, or Ireland, there's a ton of this going on. Some CEOs have publicly declared that outsourcing is a non-negotiable fact of life for American businesses. If lower-end workers in the United States experience "dislocations" from all the "restructuring," well, that's just the way it is. It's an "absolute necessity."

We believe in outsourcing at Beryl because it's what we do. But we do it all here in the United States, because we think the concept of doing it offshore, though attractive in some cases, would be far more detrimental to our status as a premium provider.

Seventy-five percent of Beryl's cost is labor, and labor is clearly cheaper in Manila. The simple business proposition is that we could fatten up our margins by dumping the three hundred coworkers on our Texas crew. I won't do that for a number of reasons. By far the most important factor is my commitment to the people who work right here in the suburb of Bedford, Texas, and my dedication to their families. It would be worse than hypocritical of me to have built up and touched these families and then to shut the whole outfit down in order to make a quicker buck. I just don't believe in doing things like that. I believe it's absolutely necessary for me to stay loyal to the people who work here today and got us here in the first place.

It's really worth noting that most of the people who outsource offshore—the "corporate flight" companies that are criticized for abandoning the American worker—compete in commodity businesses. Dell outsourcing its help desk was just basic commodity work. But the lure of cheap labor has much less appeal to successful premium providers. They have established themselves through hard work and demonstrable quality, and they can make a decent margin without exploiting radical wage differences. Their biggest concern is finding the absolute best people who have the passion and who are going to deliver world-class customer service. For the kind of work Beryl does, I don't believe that's achievable in an offshore environment.

I actually kind of chuckle when I see that more and more firms are learning that life offshore isn't all it was cracked up to be. The raw numbers of companies giving it a shot may be increasing, but a number of the early adopters are finding out that they're not really saving the kind of money they planned, or delivering the quality they expected.

I'm all for globalization and running a profitable business. But rather than try to capitalize on a fad with all the other commodity businesses, Beryl will continue to make long-term investments in the culture and in the loyal coworkers who earned us our freedom to begin with.

MELANIE'S STORY

I'd had five jobs in two years and my husband's company was going through a reorganization, so I needed another part-time job. When I first started working the night shift at Beryl, naturally I wondered what the owners would be like.

Paul, Mark, and Barry showed up at two in the morning after a flight from Los Angeles. After they changed clothes and played roller hockey in the parking lot, they came in and skated around the cubicles so they could visit with the night crew. That right there took the intimidation level away. You see these three guys growing a business, who have a strong bond as brothers, and who don't treat you as employees.

And it was a surprise.

I'll be here ten hours a day and come back in the evening just to water the plants. Or to put the chairs back in place on the patio. For me, it's a sense of pride. I feel like Beryl is mine. It's not mine, of course, but I have such a sense of pride that I take ownership of things that need to be done. It wouldn't bother me a bit if somebody needed something vacuumed or dusted. I'd just do it. Because that's what you do for something you love.

Melanie is a team leader who has been with the company for ten years.

CHAPTER FOUR:

IT'S ALL ABOUT CULTURE

W hy "do" culture at all? What's the point?

My brothers and I never set out to do it. And we'd been doing it for more than a dozen years before we even knew there was a word for it. We always sensed that how we treated our people made a big difference, but we didn't start building up a program systematically until we saw the direct results in the bottom line. After five years of double digit revenue increases and a triple digit surge in profits, we're building on it with a vengeance today.

Beryl doesn't have a fancy culture theory. As is the case with our customer service approach, I believe it's simply the combination of little things we do that make our coworkers smile on the job and at home. This book gets its title from the question I hear every week from customers and visitors who walk through our facility for the first time. To us the work environment seems normal, but outsiders find the place radically upbeat. They always ask why everyone is smiling.

Here's a roster of practical tactics and programs that have helped Beryl management create the smiles that we know created the great numbers mentioned earlier. Variants of them, applied consistently, can help turn almost any commodity business into a place where people really like to work, which is, sadly, almost never the case these days.

PHYSICAL ENVIRONMENT

A FREQUENTLY OVERLOOKED NO-BRAINER. Every workplace, fundamentally, is just a place. It may be possible to build a gorgeous culture in an ugly place, but I think it would be an uphill battle.

Many visitors to our facility talk about the feeling or "vibe" they experience the minute they physically walk through the doors. We get a lot of comments on everything from space planning to fabrics to displays. Our expansive open areas create a dynamic team environment, and the low-walled cubicles let people see one another and interact. We have the ideal mix of bright colors and calming light. "Pink noise" technology in the ceiling muffles the buzz of voices and helps advisors relax.

There's a futuristic central display console hanging down from the ceiling like an arena scoreboard. It has flat screens that tell people exactly what's going on in terms of call activity. More flat screens in the lobby and break room alert coworkers to client tours, internal events, and staff birthdays. Even our bathrooms are nicely appointed and scrupulously maintained. We pipe in the same kind of classical and jazz music you'd normally hear in fine restaurants.

PERSONAL RECOGNITION

THE EMOTIONAL ENVIRONMENT IS WHERE CULTURE IS BUILT, and Beryl lays the foundation with personal recognition. For years now, I've kept a stack of note cards on my desk, and I write personal note cards every day. I do this for customers and other business people I meet, but the primary use is for coworker recognition.

On every anniversary of every coworker's start date with Beryl, I'll write a card thanking them and congratulating them for however many years of service they've given the company. I reflect on something a little bit personal or related to their jobs. I know most of the people here, but we have a system in place that can feed me up-to-date information on the rare person I haven't had a chance to talk with recently. If a coworker just got married or engaged, I'll know about it. The human resources department also makes sure that I get current notes about the hobbies or leisure pursuits that matter most to each card recipient.

If a coworker coaches his son's baseball team, his note card may read, "Your first year at Beryl made a huge difference to the project management team. And congratulations on taking the Mustangs all the way to the T-ball semifinals last month!" The important thing is to make a connection in a way that shows that I know them and that I follow their careers and families with interest. In most cases I already do, but the system makes sure I'm consistent and nobody slips through the cracks. Here's another coworker e-mail:

Amy M. (11/28/05)
Subject: Condolence Note

Dear Paul:
Late last week I received the card that you sent me in regards to
the loss of my mother. I just wanted to let you know that I truly appre-
ciate your kind words. I especially appreciated your note because even
though you are still in the grieving process yourself, you took the time
to make sure that I knew I was being thought of and supported.

I probably send out fifty of these note cards to coworkers every month. Until I started doing it, I would never have believed the impact such a gesture could make. If you walk through our facility today you will see dozens of these cards pinned up on cubicles and office walls everywhere. Sometimes I'll send them to the coworker's home address; sometimes I'll send them to spouses, thanking them for allowing their partner to work with us and describing the terrific contribution their husband or wife makes to our business. It takes less than a minute to write a note and the goodwill it creates lasts for years.

HELPING THOSE IN NEED

BERYL STARTED AS A FAMILY BUSINESS and we readily extend that family sensibility to everybody working with us. Reaching out to distressed coworkers is what we do. It's definitely not a case of me taking care of them—the program is not a paternal or hierarchical thing. The idea is that everybody in the company needs to take care of one another in a true "family style" support network.

BerylCares is the name of the behind-the-scenes program that gathers information about events in a coworker's life. We can't recognize births, weddings, and other joyful happenings and then turn a blind eye to personal calamities. Instead, we reach out very quickly if somebody is going through a rough time due to a health situation, a death in the family, or just a patch of rotten luck. If there's anything we can do as a company to help and support them, we want to know about it and acknowledge it. I am notified of each case and can do any number of things: write a note card, call someone, make a hospital visit, or attend a funeral. If our culture preaches taking care of our own, the caring has to start in my office.

All of these outreaches are memorable and they emotionally impact me as well as the people in distress. Not too long ago, a coworker got his knee crushed in a car accident. Our COO and I went to see him in the hospital and found out that his glasses got smashed in the wreck, too. The poor guy couldn't tell who we were until he heard our voices, and he was having a hard time getting food from his dinner plate into his mouth. He was too preoccupied with all the pain in his leg to even think about his glasses, so we asked HR to see what they could do. Somehow they tracked down the prescription, and with the help of a few coworkers on this team, they managed to get him a new pair the next day. This is such an important part of our culture that we've scattered similar stories throughout the book.

I think the *BerylCares* program grew out of simple acts of kindness that we just used to do instinctively in the early days. When we were commuting back and forth from Los Angeles, for example, we were always landing in Dallas after midnight. We made it a point to stop in and say hello to people on the night shift. We'd bring them pizzas and soft drinks. My brothers and I had worked a lot of those graveyard shifts before, and we knew that things like that meant a lot at three in the morning.

BerylCares is designed to make sure nobody gets overlooked. We have an internal Web site that managers can use to submit information about the personal lives of coworkers. This allows senior management to reach out and make meaningful connections. When they see senior management focused on coworker recognition, they follow suit. This has the added advantage of sending a clear warning to any old-school types who might otherwise try to manage by fear or intimidation.

The results of these outreach efforts are very rewarding. A trainer just reminded me that I'd called him on a Sunday two years ago to make sure he was doing all right after a nasty kidney stone. I'd almost forgotten the call, but it obviously meant something to him. I've called people on their cell phone the day they were getting ready to take long emergency leaves and told them not to worry about their jobs. We did a trivial thing, years ago, for one coworker who still doesn't stop thanking me with tears in his eyes. Like the note cards, these little good deeds are easy to do and mean the world to the person on the receiving end. Here's an excerpt from an e-mail to our HR director from a call advisor who had just given birth to a child after the father abandoned her:

I got a really nice "happy anniversary" note from Paul in the mail last night. He told me that he "knows I have had some tough times lately, but to be positive and everything will be OK." That was so unexpected and so welcomed. It brought tears to my eyes. Thank you all for being there for me.

Beryl is a for-profit business, not a charity. But as part of our extended family philosophy, we have dispensed emergency financial help, bought school clothes for kids, and occasionally paid rent for coworkers in distress. When the neediness seems to stem from lifestyle or poor judgment, we've had a lot of success in helping people change behaviors and move in the direction of a long-term solution.

MAKING IT FUN

YOU CAN'T HAVE A GOOD CULTURE WITHOUT HAVING FUN. We believe that so strongly that our human resources group is formally titled the "Department of Great People and Fun." Beryl conducts many events throughout the year expressly for that purpose. On the simple side, we have themes like "Dress the '70s" and "Pajama Day" and "Crazy Hat Day." On "Movie Night," we'll take fifty to a hundred people to a local cinema tavern that serves dinner. On "Ranger Night," we'll take another big group to watch the local major league baseball team. Our schedule is always changing and usually packed, and people really get into these events.

On the more elaborate side, we have an annual "Gong Show." This extremely popular talent contest allows people to show off their gifts, real or imaginary. One of the prize categories is "Most Painful to Watch," and, for me, these acts are often the most fun to watch. We also did a very challenging six-week "Survivor" competition that gave people a chance to earn a trip to New York to visit an important client. This meant a lot to many of our folks who had never been out of Texas. In "March Madness," the COO and I defied any two people in the company to beat us at two-on-two basketball. The tournament ran over the course of four weeks and we ultimately lost in the finals, which is always great for morale.

When management shows its fun side, the whole organization breathes easier. As I mentioned earlier, every year we create comic videos for our holiday party that depict senior leadership in embarrassing or compromising predicaments. This tradition makes everyone realize that there is no class system—or caste system—at Beryl. We don't need any senior executives that are too uptight about their status and image to walk around all day wearing baby bonnets. My brother Barry was game for repeated dunkings in a carnival water tank by crowds of baseball-flinging coworkers who shrieked with delight the whole time. I have taken pies in the face and have been forced to perform wacky dance routines in a lime green leisure suit and a goofy red wig.

Did this undermine anybody's authority? On the contrary, it underscored the fact that we're all just human beings here and we're all going to work together, enjoy one another's friendship, and have a good time.

The last time I spoke to an MBA class about Beryl, students from companies like Lockheed Martin and Burlington Northern Santa Fe were strongly questioning the feasibility of doing all this stuff while trying to run a practical business operation. One student had some call center management experience and knew how important it was that companies like ours keep people on the phones to maintain service levels. He was particularly challenging about what he kind of derisively called "the strategy of fun." I told everybody, "Look, I don't run a theme park. First and foremost, we're in business to make money and perform. But we do have technologies that allow us to monitor performance and schedule people in a way that makes smart use of culture, training, and development. And they pay off for us in a big way in terms of dollars." I think they got the message.

At all these events, the power of food helps strengthen the sense of community. It seems that not a day goes by where we're not either having some kind of potluck event or bringing in food. This always adds to the atmosphere and sense of camaraderie.

LaToija J. (6/14/06)
Subject: We Appreciate You!

Paul:

I just wanted to say that we appreciate all that you and [Chief Operating Officer] Lance [Shipp] have done lately. It's not easy, but you have done great with meeting the needs of your employees. The decorations are beautiful; the restroom at the main entrance is stunning and smells great! We appreciate the reimbursements, the Town Hall meetings, the Beryl Well meetings, the Health Fairs, the Family Gatherings and parties, Movie Night, etc, etc. Bless you and the family. This e-mail is only to express our appreciation because everyone needs to know they are appreciated every once in a while.

Even little things like job titles can enliven a culture. We don't hesitate to play with titles because we've always looked at ourselves as a very flat organization where titles don't mean a lot. Our receptionist's title is Director of First Impressions. The person who heads up the Department of Great People and Fun—usually called HR—is the Queen of Fun and Laughter.

So whether you're looking for a job at Beryl or walking in through the door for the first time, we deliver the messages up front that (a) this is a fun and special place, and (b) if you do come on board, you're going to see that throughout your experience here.

INTEGRATING WITH FAMILIES

I FREQUENTLY HEAR FROM SPOUSES that they benefit at home from the sense of fulfillment their husband or wife has found at Beryl. This means a lot to me, and over time, we've learned to proactively involve the families of everybody who works here. The first thing I do when I stand up to welcome people to the annual holiday party is to thank all the spouses for allowing their partners or significant others to spend a good part of their lives with Beryl. The more we integrate families into what we do, the more we enrich the lives of our coworkers and their loved ones.

Cindy P. (11/31/03)
Subject: Monthly CEO Letter

Paul:
Thanks for the words of encouragement, direction, and motivation. I'm so very pleased to be working at a company whose executives value their employees so much. I overheard my husband, Tim, telling a friend of ours last weekend what a change in attitude I have had since working here. He said he can tell how much I love it here.

For our annual Family Day, we close down our parking lot and build a carnival with rides and games. This year we had about five hundred people. It was, as always, a big event for folks who may not get a chance to go out very often to do things with their kids.

We try to do something special every Family Day. I had a Camry with very low mileage and was getting ready to sell it when the idea came to me that we should give it away at Family Day. I wanted to make sure we gave it to somebody who needed it, but also somebody who exemplified the Beryl values. So we had a contest where people could write a one-thousand word essay to nominate someone they felt deserved the car.

There were a lot of great and funny stories, but only one person received multiple nominations. Unbeknownst to all but those who nominated him, he had been walking to work for seven months: seven miles each way, fourteen miles a day. In spite of thunderstorms and one-hundred-degree heat, he never missed a day and wasn't late once. Throughout the seven months, he never told anybody about it. If he hadn't dropped forty pounds, nobody might ever have noticed. Why was he suffering through all this? Because his mom's car had broken down and he gave her his car so she could get to work.

On Family Day, after we announced the runners up, we called out the winner's name to great fanfare. He came up and immediately broke into tears. When I gave him the keys to the car, he gave me a huge hug and didn't want to let go. The general effect on the whole crowd couldn't have been better.

La Toya R. (5/22/06)
Subject: Family Day

Good morning, Paul. After Family Day my son said, "Your company is always giving away things to people, it's like being on Oprah!" I assured him that the more you give, the more you receive.

Our company magazine is another great tool that's helped us bond with families. *Beryl Life* goes out to our coworkers' homes once a month and it's designed specifically to be read by family members. There are stories for kids, puzzles, and pictures to color. We do the magazine completely in-house, and the group responsible takes a great deal of pride in it.

"Breakfast with Santa" is the latest smash hit in the family integration program.

One Saturday morning last year I put the whole Santa costume on and sat in the break room for three hours while a long line of kids told me what they wanted for Christmas. We had games, arts and crafts, cookies, and a professional photographer to make sure every child got a picture with Santa. It meant the world to the kids and their moms and dads and that meant a lot to me.

Tracey C. (12/17/05)
Subject: Get Ready, Santa!

Paul:

Today should be fun! Hope you're ready for it! I think we're up to about one hundred kids now. Time to make the donuts!

EVANGELIZING THE VALUES

IN THE EARLY DAYS OF THE BUSINESS I was very cynical about mission statements. I never really understood them or believed that they had a tangible impact. However, after a while, I realized that it would be much easier for coworkers to make daily decisions if the company had a simple code of ethics. A large group of people got together and hammered out a value system over the course of many long discussions. Once we rolled that code out, I was impressed at how quickly the new value system became a part of our culture. These are the values we named:

- Passion for customer service
- Never sacrificing quality
- Always doing the right thing
- Spirit of camaraderie

You can walk out onto the call center floor and ask any advisor what the official company values are and he or she will be able to tell you. They often analyze day-to-day decisions according to those values. Faced by a tough choice in some business situation, we might simply say, "Are we doing the right thing?" Generally, this just means, "Are we taking the high road and demonstrating integrity?"

The idea of "never sacrificing quality" has been especially handy because our clients are always trying to get us to do things we've never done before. This value enables us to turn away business comfortably in situations where we think we wouldn't be able to live up to our standards as a quality provider.

When people have these rules of thumb in front of them on their desks, it helps them keep their decisions contained and helps Beryl grow its business in a more disciplined way. The values have become so important they're actually part of our performance appraisal process. You get graded annually on your adherence to the values and they become part of your bonus potential.

People have actually lost their jobs for ignoring the values. One woman stole a brilliant, innovative idea from a coworker and presented it to a supervisor as her own. She took the credit and the praise, and we had to let her go because that kind of integrity-free maneuvering may be common practice elsewhere, but it's just not the right thing to do at Beryl.

Sandy R. (9/16/05)
Subject: The Beryl Difference

Paul:

I wanted to tell you the story of how I came to Beryl. At the beginning of 2001, I had a job I loved and a boss I loved. Then that company filed for bankruptcy. Being in the accounting department, I saw the ugly truth. The owners and upper management showed their true colors as the company fell apart. Well, it didn't take long to realize the Beryl difference. This company is so successful and blessed because of the values that you three brothers founded it on. You have integrity, a respect for your employees, and a love for all people.

SUCCESSFUL CULTURE PROGRAMS

HAVING PEOPLE RECOGNIZE THEIR PEERS is a big part of our spirit of camaraderie. Our PRIDE@Beryl program lets coworkers praise others for living one or more of the Beryl values or for doing something extra special. It stands for Peers Recognizing Individual Deeds of Excellence. They submit the event on an internal Web site to generate a certificate for the person being recognized. The certificate is presented by the recipient's supervisor and specifies which value was honored and in what way. The recipient generally displays it around his or her desk for others to see. Once a month we reward four coworkers with special parking spaces, each being recognized for living one of the four Beryl values.

Once a quarter, we have a contest to pick one Pride certificate recipient for a $1,000 prize. The prize isn't straight cash, per se, because it's important to us that the winners end up with something tangible as a result of their good deeds. Before we hand over the money, we ask the winner to specify what he or she intends to purchase with it for himself or herself and/or his or her family. Winners have bought furniture, stereos, and trips. Feedback we've received tends to corroborate that this approach makes a more meaningful and lasting impression on the winner than if he or she just uses the cash to pay bills.

BETTER BERYL BUREAU

CULTURE IS SOMETHING PEOPLE CREATE at all levels of the organization and cannot be something simply mandated by senior executives, so we use committees to involve as many coworkers as possible. Our main culture committee decided to call itself the Better Beryl Bureau. They took the job very seriously and made it clear early on that the focus of the BBB was not going to be "fun." They wanted to work on enhancing and improving the culture through a wide variety of practical applications, some of them fairly sophisticated.

The first thing these fifteen people looked at was our method of coworker orientation. They completely revamped this "on-boarding" process to make it much more impactful. Now when new coworkers start, a large group of people welcome each individual at the door on their first day to get the person pumped up and feeling important. The BBB also put together a "Right Start" program that allows every new coworker to spend time with all the different managers in the company during their first couple of weeks. Right Start has been very effective in teaching new coworkers what we do, why we do it, and what their specific role is going to be.

Because of its impressive record of achievements, the BBB has become a powerful group and a real shaper of life at Beryl. If any issues or decisions are pending that might affect the culture, senior management consults with the BBB.

MANAGEMENT COMMUNICATIONS COUNCIL

THIS COMMITTEE IS SIX OR SEVEN PEOPLE, all of them call advisors elected by their peers. The idea is to open up communications between senior leaders and the large group of coworkers who take the calls. There are lots of forums for communication at Beryl, but we want to make sure these critically important folks have their own place where they can talk about what they need and then receive feedback.

This group gets together on a regular basis and their issues run the gamut. It could be a little thing, like wanting water fountains in the middle of the call center floor so coworkers don't have to walk all the way to the break room. It could be a big thing, like the matter of compensation. From a salary standpoint, Beryl is not the highest-paying company in the industry, but our total compensation, our benefits, and overall environment make for a highly competitive package. That's one reason our retention rate is so much higher than those of similar companies.

When the MCC brought the issue to us, we spent a lot of time teaching the representatives how to understand and interpret the compensation issues so they could bring a sense of understanding to the larger call advisor group. Here's an e-mail excerpt from a call advisor to her supervisor that indicates the messaging is sinking in:

The jobs I have worked for in the past were paying way below the rate of other companies. Here at Beryl, the employees are paid at a great rate and the rate matches the work that is done. Also, the rates do not stay the same; the rates increase as long as the employees are employed with Beryl. Employees are awarded with raises as long as their performance is great. If Beryl profits, the employees profit. I like the idea of that.

BERYL WELL

A LOT OF PEOPLE IN TEXAS think that because I came from California I only eat avocados and sprouts. Fitness is important to me; I'm just not particularly good at it! I've always had to battle my weight and fight to stay in shape. I know what it's like to eat a hot fudge sundae and feel terrible about it the next day.

When I came to Texas, I must admit that I thought the emphasis on fitness wasn't as prevalent or as high as it was in

California. This was probably even truer in a call center environment where people don't have to worry about being seen by the public. I got an insight when a coworker complained to me about the "dress nice" days we schedule when we're expecting special visitors. She said, "Why does it matter what we look like? We work here because we don't want people to see us."

I understood her fear of critical eyes because I've been twenty-five pounds heavier than I am now. When my former girlfriend told me she didn't care what I looked like, I thought, *"Well, guess what? I'm vain and I do!"* And when I didn't feel good about myself, I didn't want to participate in things, either. So when I see people who aren't in shape and who are unhappy about it, I know that if we encourage them to take better care of themselves, they can lead happier and more productive lives. I also know that healthy, happy, productive, confident people are better for our business.

Developing a great wellness program that stuck became a personal challenge for me. There are lots of structured programs out there, but we decided to do ours on our own. Beryl Well is based on a simple commitment. Each coworker signs a contract with herself or himself to improve his or her health and fitness in one specific way or another. It can be to lose weight, do more exercise, quit smoking—or any other goal they can measure.

About a third of the company signed up proactively. We appointed coaches to work with people who chose to be on their teams. I'm one of the coaches and I meet with members individually to understand their personal goals, challenges, and what they're trying to achieve. Everybody knows I'm not a nutritionist or a certified trainer. Nobody cares. These people are just looking for support. Here's what one wrote:

Paul:

I wanted to thank you for meeting with me on Wednesday. I had become discouraged after weighing on Friday and binged a little. Speaking with you allowed me to refocus and set a few small goals that will help my overall progress toward a lifestyle adjustment. Here are a few changes I wanted you to know about:

1. *I have begun eating Honey Bunches of Oats w/skim milk for breakfast (I couldn't just jump right into the Grapenuts).*

2. *I have drank 88oz of water each day since our meeting.*

3. *I called Rodney at 24hr Fitness and scheduled an "intake" for this afternoon.*

Again, I just wanted to thank you for your suggestions and support of a program that encourages me to take care of myself.

The team gets together once a month. Again, I'm really just a facilitator to help them talk and share stories about whatever issues they're up against. It could be a cool gym somebody found or a quick, healthy recipe for fish. When I think about my day, it's really wonderful to me that I can be on the phone doing some fairly high-level deal-making and then, five minutes later, be sitting in one of these meetings next to a call advisor, asking her how many glasses of water she's had to drink that day or what she had for breakfast. I've found that it's the basics people really need to understand, simple things like drinking lots of water and eating breakfast. I've been told a million times that Chicken McNuggets are super-healthy because they're chicken. This was the biggest "a-hah!" for me, the fact that people did not even know how to make healthy choices.

Making smart choices is hard to do in a sedentary job where it's easy to get up from your seat and go to the vending machines. To make sure there are healthy choices in the machines, we've had to do a little arm-twisting with the vendors, who just want to fill the machines with junk that sells. Cost is very important to our staff, so three times a week we arrange for caterers to come in and sell inexpensive food like wraps, soups, and salads. At every event where food is provided, a healthy option is always available.

Every Monday morning at eight o'clock, we put out fresh fruit, yogurt, nuts, raisins, and all kinds of other healthy fare. The idea is to kick the week off with a big, free, smart breakfast for the whole company. The first time the idea was suggested, the reaction was, "Paul, it's going to be a real hassle to go to the store and get big bags of apples and bananas." There was also a perception that we'd never be able to wean the majority of our people away from their usual breakfast of sausage, egg and cheese McMuffins, washed down with Mountain Dew.

Today, if we tried to take away the healthy Monday breakfast, there would be an ugly riot in the lounge. The biggest problem now is people eating all the granola right away and not leaving enough for people who come in later. I think the net result of this weekly feeding frenzy is that everybody has gotten the message that getting a healthy start on the day and the week is important. Here's an example:

Paul:
Thanks for the free healthy food on Mondays. That is a very nice touch which I have never seen before in any of the companies I have worked for. They have often paid lip service to things like that,

but never actually practiced what they preached. You guys rock. You follow through with actions that back up your words.

Beryl Well is designed for people at all stages of fitness savvy. One coworker wanted to get fit but couldn't afford to join a gym, so every weekend she was taking her kids to Wal-Mart and walking laps around the aisles for two hours. To help guide other people on tight budgets, we hired a gym to bring in speakers once a month on subjects like exercise, weight loss, and nutrition. We also coordinate a lot of activities like 5K runs and walks to ensure that people who can't afford a gym have ways to participate. And if people go to the gym and track their visits, we'll pay for it.

Julia C. (4/6/06)
Subject: Thank You

Paul:
Thank you so much for this health fair. I was going to go outside to smoke but decided to stay at the health fair instead. You stopped me from having one less cigarette. I ate some veggies and fruit instead of having a cigarette. I'm sweating but I'm going to try to push through this morning without a cigarette! I'm excited for myself. I have a short-term personal goal to smoke one less cigarette and Beryl has helped me! Now it's on to goal two!

Of course, some people are going to do well and some people are going to struggle. Struggling together as a team is what it's all about. We knew that if we ended up with a few inspiring success stories, people who could spread the word to others, it would change lives. We've seen Stacey lose 200 pounds and keep it off. Margie won "Woman of the Year" at Curves Gym. Pat, our former CFO, who hated himself for being out of shape and lost seventy pounds, finally got bored with running marathons last year. Now he runs twenty-four-hour races and just took a trophy in his category after running 107 miles.

A lot of the success comes from creating ownership of the program. We've learned from past experience that if we keep some of these softer programs under the human resources umbrella, they don't work as well as when we spread the ownership out across the organization. Only then do they get the attention they need and have a chance to attract leaders who are truly passionate in these areas. The person currently in charge of the wellness program is our controller. Carol happens to be a diabetic for whom nutrition has been an important life-long issue. When we let it be known we were looking for a leader she stepped up and said, "I can do that!" And she's made the wellness program a phenomenal success. There is so much talent and passion in any organization. All you need to do is ask, and people will step forward.

BERYL OUTREACH

THE OTHER AREA where I think we've had some good success is called Beryl Outreach, which the company funds to support the community. We've realized that helping to take care of the local community is one of the best ways we can develop our people as individuals and our culture as a whole. This evolved over the years from simple early efforts in which we'd gather things like school supplies and Christmas gifts and deliver them.

Last year we started to think we wanted to do things in a bigger way, so we picked four different charities. For alternating three month stretches, we did everything we could to help these groups with both money and a healthy load of hands-on volunteer work. The satisfaction of giving has definitely strengthened our own sense of family and community. In 2006, we decided to focus on a single group, so we could concentrate our efforts throughout the year.

"EMPLOYER OF CHOICE"

FOR THE LAST FOUR YEARS the *Dallas Business Journal* has named Beryl one of the "Top Ten Places to Work" in the Dallas/Fort Worth market, and the Texas Department of Business has ranked us twice on their roster of best employers in the state. As this book goes to print, we await word on our nomination as one of the "Top 50 Best Small Places to Work in America." Winning these awards regularly has been very useful and important to us.

First of all, they generate great pride throughout the company. We celebrated the first award by renting a limousine and driving to the presentation luncheon with ten coworkers who had either been nominated by their peers or won a contest. I'm sure that not all these folks had sat through a fancy lunch in a big hotel ballroom before. Their reactions while the waiters served them were touching. One call advisor, who may never have owned a suit, bought one especially for the occasion. As we were riding to the hotel in the back of the limo he looked at me and said, "This is the proudest day of my life."

Public recognition of our culture has helped us recruit coworkers. Knowing we're an employer of choice makes applicants want to work here at all levels. We just made a very important senior level hire who told me she had no interest until the headhunter mentioned the awards. Finally, these awards mean a lot to our clients. If they have to outsource their customer interaction function, why not give it to the happiest workers in Texas?

Angela L. (4/24/04)
Subject: Thank You

Paul:

Thank you for the warm note you gave me about "The Best Places to Work" luncheon. I was overwhelmed by the opportunity to attend. What an honor! I truly feel what it means to work at one of the Metroplex's best places to work. That whole phrase was kind of obscure to me back when I interviewed but now that I've been here for eight months (I can't believe it. The time has flown by) it has a personal and significant meaning to me. I've worked for some good companies as well as some "dogs." CONGRATULATIONS! Get that acceptance speech ready for next year.

PHYSICAL, EMOTIONAL, SPIRITUAL

TRADITION AND CONSISTENCY are critical to the development of culture, doing things that work over and over again. When you find something that works, keep tweaking it to make it better. If you can create the sense of anticipation and excitement that we've been able to develop with crazy events like our "Gong Show," you've activated the emotional dimension that makes for truly inspired corporate culture.

Great culture is a mind and body experience. It's physical, spiritual, and, for some people, religious. Good leaders nourish their people on as many levels as possible. And you'll be surprised at the nourishment you receive in return when calamity strikes close to home.

In 2005, my brother Barry passed away as a result of brain cancer. It was incredible how much everyone rallied around me and around one another. For the last three months of Barry's illness, particularly when I needed to spend less and less time at the company, people who had worked with him and me for years really overwhelmed us with support.

Professionally, I knew the business was going to be taken care of. Everybody, without exception, stepped up the same commitment and dedication they always had and said, "We've got you covered." So I never had to worry about the train jumping the tracks. Secondly, the looks, words, and hugs I'd get when I was in the building gave me a special comfort. There was a Web site called a Care Page that I set up to communicate Barry's status at any point in time. This site allowed people to post messages to one other and to the person who is sick. The comments we got from Beryl coworkers were incredibly heartwarming.

Tim G. (9/8/05)

Dear Barry:

Thanks for being my boss.

Thanks for being my friend.

Thanks for always calling me out.

Thanks for making fun of me.

Thanks for giving me the opportunity to respond, even if I am never quick enough.

Thanks for never taking the little things too serious.

Thanks for beating me in golf.

Thanks for inviting me into your home.

Thanks for showing me how to be a loving father and using words like "sweetie" when talking to your sons.

Thanks for taking the time, even if brief.

Thanks for hanging up the phone quickly, but calling back to ask for more.

Thanks for rarely giving in.

Thanks for being like a brother.

Thanks for being my friend.

There were two occasions that really showed me how special the people here are. In one case, about a month or so before Barry died, coworkers decided to hold a prayer vigil. They set up in our "quiet room" and I brought my parents, who were staying in town. People just started getting up and talking about what Barry meant to them, sharing their thoughts and prayers with my parents. It was the most amazing thing and ended up with an exceptionally gifted vocalist singing "Amazing Grace." There wasn't a dry eye in the place. To know that, in their own way, people were hurting as much as I was and as much as my parents were just blew us away.

When Barry died, we had the funeral in Los Angeles, but it was important to me that the coworkers here who were so close to Barry did not miss out on the ability to get some closure and celebrate his life. It was impossible for all of them to fly 1,500 miles to California, so we decided to have a service here at Beryl right in the middle of the call center floor. And for the first time in the company's history, we shut down the phones. At two o'clock that afternoon, the Beryl phones went silent.

Everybody gathered around and sat on the floor. Lots of former coworkers came, people I hadn't seen in years who were very close to my brother. People spoke, people sang. I was given a wonderful bracelet that said "For Barry" on it, with "In loving memory" on the back, something I cherish and always will. That day everything I'd ever tried to do for our people was returned to me and more.

Debbie M. (1/09/06)
Subject: Thank You

Paul:

I was very saddened when Barry passed away and I still include you and your family in my prayers. I worked the graveyard shift when I was first hired and I can remember Barry stopping in many times at night and chatting with us late-nighters (since we didn't have many visitors, it was always hard to get away!), and we enjoyed that. One of the things I remember about Barry and his humor was when I had worked the night before and had to run to the Tom Thumb in

Bedford looking like I had just gotten out of bed. I was in the frozen food section, and when I looked over, guess who was standing right next to me? Barry! I apologized and apologized for having no makeup on and for wearing the same clothes I had worked in the night before. Barry looked at me and smiled and said that he wouldn't tell anyone if I didn't tell anyone he was there in his sweats! We both laughed. I really miss seeing Barry here and want to thank you for taking time prior to his passing to make sure we were all included.

MICHAEL'S STORY:

My mom was diagnosed with cancer very late and they didn't give her long to live. I couldn't afford to fly home at the time, so Paul wasted no time buying my airplane ticket and sending me home so I could spend the last month with my mom before she died.

The whole time I was there, my coworkers donated their vacation and personal time so I could stay. Everybody just kept telling me, "Don't worry about it. You need to be there, family comes first."

I could never, ever expect that from anybody else or even try to repay it, you know. It was very fortunate that I was able to be there when my mom passed away. I love them to death for that and I'll never leave.

Michael is in charge of facilities and security at Beryl, with previous experience in fulfillment. He is a member of the Better Beryl Bureau.

CHAPTER FIVE:

LEADERSHIP SECRETS

When my brothers and I started the business, there were only the three of us. Today, I'm the lone remaining founder. As Beryl's CEO, people inside and outside of the company look to me as "the guy." The road to my becoming CEO had a few surprising turns.

The dynamics between my brothers and me were unusually positive. There was never a pecking order or competition. We had different talents and interests that complemented each other. So for years, there was no real need for a clear-cut leader. Besides, the three of us were almost always too busy to worry about who was in charge! After we took over the Texas operation, our schedules became especially brutal. Commuting every week back and forth from Dallas deprived us of any normal social life. The fact that Mark and I both married flight attendants hints at how wrapped up we were in the business.

Once we started hiring people, we graduated into the leadership ranks together. Over time, we went through different phases of who led what portions of the business. Mark was the obvious choice to run anything that had to do with technology. Barry handled operations, and I focused on sales and marketing. This "three chefs in the kitchen" approach worked great. We could discuss and argue our way to consensus on almost any issue. The beauty of working with family was the absolute trust and respect we had for one another.

But Beryl kept getting bigger and we couldn't keep winging it like this forever. We finally reached a point where we needed some kind of organization chart to bring clarity to our roles and to the people who looked to us for direction. No matter how ideal a genetically-linked triumvirate seemed in theory, we all knew in our guts that at some point, something had to change. Beryl was in a complex market and at a size and intensity of activity where big decisions frequently needed to be made quickly. We couldn't always get the consensus we needed as fast as we needed it to grow what we wanted to grow. It was hard for everybody not to have a single leader, and it was dangerous for the company.

None of us individually had the guts to do something about this, nor would we have agreed on what should be done. So we just kept about our business until events changed the way we governed the company. It didn't really happen by design.

The equation shifted when my older brother left Beryl in 2000. Mark had been the undisputed architect of our first venture together. An active entrepreneur before throwing in with me and Barry, he was a non-stop idea man who frequently looked at other opportunities. As much as he loved Beryl and working with us, he decided he wanted to take advantage of a chance to do something different and left to start another business.

While it was difficult for Barry and me to accept this at the time, it was very likely the best thing that could have happened for all of us, not only in terms of our relationship, but in terms of the company moving forward. Mark continues to work with Beryl with the business he's in now, and Beryl benefits tremendously from the unique technology he develops.

When Mark left, Barry didn't want to be "the guy." He felt very comfortable being responsible for certain functional aspects of the operation, and with me taking the helm as CEO. Fifteen years after we all started together, I was sole leader. It was an opportunity I took on with great passion, and one that I knew very little about. I didn't go to CEO school and had never worked for other companies, so I lacked any theoretical frames of reference for what good leadership means. What I knew, I'd learned through experience.

I'm still learning every day by closely observing accomplished colleagues and by reading up on anything and everything that applies. When I try to define what leadership is—and how a neophyte might start to pull it off—a few points come to mind pretty quickly.

ME, VISION?

MY ORIGINAL CYNICISM ABOUT THINGS LIKE VALUES and mission statements extended for a long time to the concept of a corporate "vision." Eventually, it became clear to me that everybody in the company had to understand exactly where we were heading and how we were trying to get there. Without a clear vision, it's too easy for coworkers to lose sight of where they fit into the picture and what the whole exercise is about. A leader has to supply tight, cohesive answers to all questions and work hard to ensure that the answers make good sense to everybody. Constantly rearticulating the vision in new ways that keep the message fresh and convincing has been very important to our success at Beryl.

At Beryl, we have a slightly different take on vision, which other companies tend to define by looking at a time in the future and saying, "What do we want to be when we reach that point?" We consider vision to be a combination of our purpose and our values.

By purpose, we mean how we're making the world a better place, i.e., "connecting people to healthcare." That's the rallying cry for the company and continues to be to this day what defines us and makes us feel good about our labors. At the end of every day we all know we tried our level best to provide this critically important service to our customers. But it wasn't a great day unless we acted in accordance with our values—collaborating ethically and passionately to achieve the highest possible quality standards. When that happens, the daily grind does seem less like a job and more like an adventure:

Bernie B. (1/30/04)
Subject: First Week

Paul:
I feel I have to tell you a little bit about my first week at Beryl . . .
I was stunned! This company helps people. This company affects lives.
This company helps people get information for family members who

are sick. This company helps teachers get information on a disease she's just contracted. This company listens to patients' concerns about how they were treated recently at a clinic, and assists them in finding contacts that might better serve the patient's needs. This company, simply put, cares.

COMMUNICATION

A LEADER IS SOMEONE WHOSE WORDS ARE TAKEN SERIOUSLY. Growing up, I never took myself that seriously or suspected that my actions and words would be considered important some day. After I assumed a management role, it took me years to realize how much weight people were giving what I said and did. You can make a casual comment in a meeting and the next thing you know half a dozen people have dropped what they're doing and are working overtime on your idea.

There's a certain seduction to power like that. You can use it in a positive way or a negative way. You can choose words that are encouraging and complimentary, or you can choose an intimidating style. As I continue to mature as a manager, it hits me hard every day that I have an unusual opportunity to use my authority in a positive way to influence people. I continue to believe that communicating what we're doing and listening to people are the best ways to be a leader and help the business.

I remember reading in a book by Bill Marriott that the seven most important words for a leader to say are: "I don't know. What do you think?" This has proven repeatedly to be some of the best advice I've ever come across. A smart CEO may have phenomenal instincts and know the answers to 80 percent of the questions that come up. But a good leader has the tact and patience to let the answers emerge from other people. This method gives them pride of ownership. They feel like they share in the decision-making instead of always being told what to do.

It takes patience to put Marriot's advice into practice, and at first that wasn't easy for me to get used to. Your natural impulse is to take charge, and it's tempting to just say, "This is what we should do." Instead, try, "I don't know. What do you think?" You'll be surprised how many times you get the same answer you had in mind, and you've done your people a big favor psychologically. They should get to feel good about themselves and the value of their input as often as possible.

IN THEIR FACES THE RIGHT WAY

OUR INTERNAL COMMUNICATIONS PROGRAM gives me multiple ways to cycle messages and collect feedback. The "town hall" meeting format has worked especially well. Our COO and I do a very informal presentation about what's going on in the business and our goals for the year. When we talk about the vision, it's always in the context of "What does this mean for you as a call advisor or member of another functional team at Beryl?" It's really important to boil it down and to speak in those terms.

We look at the town halls as a way to explain what's happening and also to offer a forum for questions, with no limit in terms of scope or topic. Quite often we'll be challenged, and occasionally someone will raise his or her hand with a stinging complaint disguised as a question. That's perfectly OK. The events are "no holds barred," and the beauty of the odd complaint is that people walk away feeling that they can air out their grievances and ask us anything. To maximize this perception, we actively solicit e-mail questions in advance and remind people to raise concerns when they come to the meeting.

In the first years of the town hall program, we'd literally answer a hundred-plus questions, either live or in writing. Over the last few years, the number of questions has decreased, even from a larger base of coworkers. We believe that's because we're addressing and settling the issues that get raised. We know for sure that it's not because people are shy or afraid to ask. Our coworkers are quite vocal and willing to tell us what they think. So with the raw numbers going down, we believe we're probably doing something right.

Every coworker attends these quarterly town halls, and that's a big challenge for a 24/7 business like ours. The process requires four or five distinct sessions and that takes two full days. Every minute off the phones is a minute of lost revenue, so the business takes a heavy financial hit. But we're committed to sharing information and we get much greater value from fielding all the suggestions.

"CHAT 'N CHEWS"

YOU CAN'T REALLY BOND WITH INDIVIDUALS in the town hall meetings, so on a monthly basis our COO and I invite twelve to fifteen different coworkers who represent various parts of the company to have lunch with us. These "Chat 'n Chew" sessions are very informal sit-downs, strictly intended to help us all get to know one other better. As important as it is for us to be open with our guests, we've found that much of the value is in the camaraderie that develops amongst coworkers who may not have interacted much before.

We talk about things the others may not know about us personally, so people feel they can tell us anything that pops into their head. I always end the session with the question: "If there were one thing you could change or improve at Beryl, what would that be?" It feels good sometimes when people struggle to find something negative, but just by asking we've gotten a number of ideas that have had a big effect company-wide. A lot of major changes at Beryl have been sparked by these little communal meals.

OUTSIDE SPEAKERS AT MEETINGS

OUR MONTHLY BUSINESS REVIEW MEETINGS include about fifty primary managers and department representatives. Like every other company in the world, we share specific monthly results as well as trends for the year. But to punch up the energy level, we also use these meetings as a learning opportunity and bring in outside speakers to give us fresh perspectives on pertinent issues.

One month, a Southwest Airlines executive will explain the nuts and bolts of that company's culture. The next month a local MBA professor will brief us on management philosophy, or we'll bring in someone from the local charity we support to share human interest stories. I get great feedback on the outside speakers. People actually look forward to these meetings.

Teresa W. (12/17/03)
Subject: Thank You

Paul and Barry:
That speaker you brought in this morning was wonderful, rein-
forcing some of my beliefs and shedding a new light on some that have
been in the shadows. Thank you for thinking about us and investing in
our futures by providing learning and growth opportunities for us.

"ASK PAUL"

WE MAXIMIZE THE NUMBER OF CHANNELS available to coworkers
who may want to get in management's face either personally or
through mediated forums. One of our most popular intranet
functions is called "Ask Paul." It's an advice column knock-off
where anybody can send a question to me that will be answered
in the next issue of our magazine for coworkers and their families.
Most of these are proper requests for information on change or
policy or the outlook for the future, but I also get some pretty
funny tongue-in-cheek letters. I'm not a comedian by any stretch
of the imagination, but I do my best to respond in kind.

In a recent question I was teased for "standing by and doing
nothing" to investigate the prank "kidnapping" of a hula dancer
statue from one executive's office. Some of the call advisors had
apparently snatched this gaudy Hawaiian tourist memento and
were holding it for ransom. The question was how could I turn
a blind eye to the desecration of this beloved Beryl icon? So I
bantered back:

Sometimes it is better not to know what your leader is doing.

Though I have been thousands of miles away during this ordeal, rest assured that I have been in contact with the key players, a hostage negotiator, our outside legal counsel, and the Employee Assistance Program to ensure the safety and stability of our coworkers during this crisis. Bottom line is that we don't negotiate with terrorists, but in this situation, everyone involved works for Beryl and we must seek a win-win solution. Please know that, as usual, I have your back.

Frivolous stuff indeed, but it shows people that I'm not the kind of distant, stuffed-shirt "power from on high" that most of them are apparently used to working for. Again, it's a weak and self-important human being who is too busy to share a laugh and who can't take a good-natured ribbing.

FLOOR TOURS

FLOOR TOURS ARE ANOTHER EXAMPLE of personal communications that are a little more in line with my personal note card approach. Several times a month, I pop down onto the call center floor with no particular agenda other than to say hello and visit with coworkers.

I'll ask advisors to get off the phone for a few minutes and just chat. The time investment is nothing compared to the impact the exposure has on the company's reputation for an "open" culture. The reactions I get, usually second and third hand, are typically people saying: "I've never been in a place where the owner will actually show up and say 'Hi!' to us or care enough to ask how we're doing."

Three brothers get started in the big hair decade of the '80s, . . .

. . . and now the state-of-the-art of the 21st century.

EMERGENCY RESPONSE SYSTEM–

help at the push of a button

EMERGENCY RESPONSE SYSTEMS, INC.

Our first brochure with Mom as our model.

A sure way to reduce stress in the call center.

Even our healthcare clients are happy to get into the act.

The COO and CEO at play.

Giving away my car to Eric, who used to walk seven miles to work.

During our annual March Madness tournament,
Jared makes it look easy.

That's Lara, whose official title is "Queen of Fun and Laughter."

Our annual gong show brings out Garth and Wayne.

A requirement of any manager at Beryl—willingness to get in the dunk tank.

Beryl Kids doing karaoke during our annual Family Day.

Prism Project

*Internal branding is just as important as what you brand
in the marketplace.*

For someone who is not a natural-born schmoozer, this required growth on my part, and initially, it was a bit of a struggle. Not that I don't enjoy the experience, but at first it was just plain hard to make the time commitment and book the tours into my schedule. Working on deals and building the business has always been easier for me than checking in on people and making what I used to consider "small talk."

Now that I've done a bunch of floor tours, they are always a high point of my week. I've consciously worked on my communication skills, and the more you do this, the more naturally the communication flows, and the more fulfilling the interactions become. For the people who look to you for leadership, there is no such thing as small talk. One question about their kids or a single compliment can make them feel like a million bucks. It's a crime not to use your power this way.

MONTHLY E-MAIL LETTER

ANOTHER SIMPLE TOOL THAT HELPS ME connect with the staff is a monthly personal e-mail letter that goes out to the whole company. This is a combination of personal stories, business updates, and philosophical observations.

Five years ago, the day my daughter was born, I started including a new picture of her every month. Now that we've got a son, I have two new pictures a month. I get great responses to this letter. People feel they know me a little better because I take a personal approach to it and de-emphasize the formal business aspect of the outreach.

Our COO does a similar e-mail called "Did Ya Know?" It's a hodgepodge of funny facts and interesting topics that always tie back to a current issue at Beryl and just another way to underscore the fact that the leaders are human beings. We not only have time for small talk, but we like jokes and stories, and we'll take a little time to brighten up the spirits of people who are often dealing with stressful situations on the phones and maybe in their personal lives, too.

NO SECRETS, NO BARRIERS

OUR APPROACH TO INFORMATION ACCESS IS WIDE OPEN. We post all of our monthly financials publicly and see no risk in that. The people who will understand the statements are going to ask us good questions. If we're doing well, we obviously want them to know about it. And the same holds true if we're not. We've found that if you share information through both the good and the bad times, a trust develops that encourages people to take the ride with you. To nurture that trust, we blanket everybody with thorough and honest information.

Jeanne S. (11/1/02)
Subject: Our Chat

Paul:

I appreciate your willingness to be up front with all employees. You made a lasting impression on me at the break room chat when you said you believe in always taking the high road. My respect for you moved to a deeper level that day . . . .

We make sure everybody knows there is no aspect of Beryl's operations in which their comments are either irrelevant or unwelcome. You can't ask your people for advice often enough, especially when you're tooling new products and services. We've been redesigning our current software system lately and have a Web site for suggestions on specific refinements and enhancements. Coworkers love the fact we're asking them and we're getting great ideas.

Regular inclusive outreaches like this are one way Beryl leaders say: "We don't know everything. What do you think?"

"WEEDING THE GARDEN"

ONE BIG ADVANTAGE I HAD IN FOUNDING THE COMPANY with my brothers was never feeling threatened in my position and never having to wage any turf battles. With no ego to guard, it's usually been pretty easy for me to see where other people have great skills and experience that I don't. A lot of leadership has to do with understanding your own limitations and building a support team around you.

When I'm lucky enough to have talented folks cross my path, it's never been a problem for me to promote them, or, if they're outsiders, to invite them aboard. I like people who know more than I do. They enhance my experience and help the company grow in ways that I could not. Over the last several years we thoroughly revamped our whole management team, moving people up from within and looking outside to find the complementary skills. I am now happily surrounded by people who are more experienced and smarter than I am.

"Weeding the garden" is the way I look at developing leadership around me. It doesn't mean firing weak performers. It means creating an environment where people with great potential can grow into peak performance. Here are a few helpful rules of thumb.

CONSTANT FEEDBACK

WE BELIEVE IN GIVING PEOPLE GOOD HONEST FEEDBACK and doing it often. Weekly one-on-one meetings are required for all direct reports. The more informal that feedback can be, and the more often we can give it, the more valuable it is. At Beryl we've gone to a quarterly review process for everybody. It's a simple sit down discussion, maybe at the end of a normal functional meeting, where a manager can ask the coworker, "What's working? What needs to be improved? How can I help you succeed?"

There's nothing particularly revolutionary about the tactic, but it allows us to stop for a minute and have a good dialogue. People feel like they're getting feedback without a formal review process that bogs them down. Annual reviews are obviously more involved, since they determine bonus and merit status.

Quarterly reviews are a discipline, another one of those little things you have to make yourself do. When we first rolled out the policy, some managers objected because they felt they were already keeping in close enough touch with their direct reports. And most of them were. But you never get as much info from casual conversation as you will in a meeting where feedback is the whole point of the exercise. We've asked our coworkers what they think about the quarterly reviews, and they've told us they want to hear their managers' perspectives as often as possible. They don't dread these sessions.

EMPTY INBOX SYNDROME

THE BIGGEST TRUISM ABOUT LEADERSHIP—and the biggest truth—is leading by example. I like a proactive team and try to inspire this quality through a behavior that has been jokingly referred to as "empty inbox syndrome." What may seem like obsessive compulsion to some has proved to be the road to greatness for many!

Philosophically, as a leader, I see myself as a traffic director. If I'm doing my job right, no task will sit on my desk for long and no one should ever be waiting for me. Why would I ever bottleneck the organization? I should have people I can delegate the task to who are empowered to do the bulk of the work. If something ends up stuck on my desk, it means I've got to fill a void. If I have to hire someone, great. One way or another, I will find a way to keep the wheels turning.

As a leader, in fact, I strive to be the single most responsive coworker in the company. When anybody needs something from me, no matter who they are, they get it immediately. When they send me an e-mail, I want them to say, "Wow, Paul is the quickest responder in the company." The coworkers are my customers and I want them to treat their customers the same way. Being Blackberry-addicted is not a virtue, but I do believe a valuable lesson is taught. Rather than do projects and be responsive when I have a chance, I'd rather be responsive and do a project when I have a chance.

Jim J. (12/30/03)
Subject: Monthly CEO Letter

Paul:

Thank you for the reminder to respond within forty-eight hours when someone says something meaningful. I've been on Beryl's payroll for about five months and I have enjoyed every minute of it. I appreciate the care and thought you put into keeping us informed, and, at least a little bit, motivated! I like getting feedback on how the company is doing. We all have a stake in the collective success of the enterprise, and it's helpful to find out how my performance impacts the company.

MENTORS

GOOD LEADERS ALSO SURROUND THEMSELVES WITH MENTORS. Some companies have a board of directors or a board of advisors. Beryl had a small advisory board a few years ago, but the one-on-one relationships I developed with the individual members turned out to be more fruitful than when I brought them together as a group.

I've maintained a group of accomplished people who I look to just to help me grow and learn. They have experience in different areas, and I can call on them freely to spend time counseling me. If I have a financial question or a people question or need a perspective on the future of the business, there's always someone I can call. Multiple opinions make for a real sounding board.

I have a great relationship with Rick Scott, the former Columbia/HCA CEO who gave my brothers and me our first big break. I made it a point to stay in touch with Rick after he left the company in 1997 because I knew the minute that I met him that his business mind operates at a stratospheric level. He basically built Columbia from nothing into a $30 billion enterprise that got him listed as one of the "Top 25 Influential People in America" by *Time* magazine.

Rick took me under his wing and started to coach me on how to bring an element of discipline into the Beryl culture. He warned me that accountability starts at the top, and since I'd been largely unsupervised my entire career I asked him if he'd mentor me in that area. Now the third Monday of every month at nine o'clock in the morning, we have a ninety minute session by phone. He holds me to an agenda that we keep developing. In this framework, he always gives me his opinions, but insists that I make all the decisions. Knowing that I have to present and defend my game plan to this outstanding thinker once a month keeps me on my toes. Rick is a very driven man whose instincts are as sharp as his mind.

In addition to everything he's taught me about business mechanics, he's also helped me learn to trust my own instincts. Rick's a big believer in moving quickly when your gut confirms a decision that needs to be made. This helped me a lot when it came to letting people go, which was something I used to agonize over. If I'd tell him there was a team member I knew wasn't going to work out, he'd push me to act.

Another very important mentor to me has been Britt Barrett, the CEO of Medical City, a large hospital in Dallas. I've learned a lot of things watching Britt operate, and it's especially inspiring to tour his facility with him. No matter where he goes in the building, cafeteria, nursing stations, or emergency room, he is greeted by coworkers with spontaneous and genuine hugs. I'd never seen anything like this before. It demonstrated a really strong and touching personal connection, and for me that's the ultimate goal of leadership.

I don't know why a leader would not develop mentor relationships. It's as simple as asking, because most people are more than willing to help. I have relationships with other mentors who've given me invaluable advice on how to build teams and get people to work together. These advisors seem to get as much out of helping as they do learning. I know that for a fact, because I've been fortunate enough now to have become a mentor to others. It's a lot of fun.

Professor John T. (6/18/05)
Subject: Presentation to My Class

Paul:

I got some great feedback from my [SMU] students and one dropped me an e-mail that said that I should definitely include you in future classes. The level of the Q & A is always an indication as to how well you connected with the students. I had a half-dozen questions myself, but I bowed to the students' curiosity.

What you can't know is how well that all fit into the timing of the course. Your efforts to create a culture and make the employees understand their part in the success of Beryl is a HUGE factor in the success of entrepreneurial companies.

We're at a point when I talk about mission, values, strategy, and tactics and how your people are an integral part of that, and a lot of the students glaze over. They've read and heard so many mission statements created by large corporations with nothing to back them that students are skeptical at best. It seems like Beryl ranks up there with Southwest and the other great service companies who live and die by their employees.

LANCE'S STORY

Before I took over operations at Beryl, I worked with a lot of emerging businesses, including INC 500 companies. Some tried to do the kind of things Beryl does, but I never felt the true sense of virtual ownership that's so common here. It was never easy for me to tie my personal values to what those other companies were doing.

I'm a CPA/MBA and really like the fact that nobody here is hung up on that kind of stuff. The way Paul taught himself is a great inspiration to our coworkers. Picking and choosing tactics from his reading, he keeps overcoming classic hurdles that bury most entrepreneurs. In the early stages, it's tough enough to navigate through the growth phase and learn to let go of certain areas of authority. Staying humble and accessible after you've done that is much, much tougher. It takes a while for some of our new senior hires to adjust if they come from places where the CEO is God and you don't dare question him. We all challenge one another here and nobody takes it personally.

When people are more focused on trying to do the right thing rather than the politically smart thing, the environment is naturally more relaxed. When there's no fear of retribution, people will take risks and say things and make proposals that would probably amount to career suicide elsewhere. How many companies pay supposedly talented people good money and then discount their advice? We'll change anything except the core values and that gives us a very solid but flexible foundation to operate from.

Our mission is to grow the business in a way that impacts peoples' lives, customers and vendors included. When you define yourself primarily as a relationship developer and see the difference these policies make on an individual's physical and spiritual health, your own emotional tank gets filled pretty regularly, too.

How many companies today practice the Golden Rule? We recently had to terminate a coworker who'd been here six years and made some important contributions. And we took a lot of time to make sure he walked away with his integrity intact, head held high. After you've worked for a few dog-eat-dog bureaucracies, it feels so much better to be working with higher ethical standards. Keeping those ethics intact as we grow is not impossible, either. We keep tweaking the culture and hiring the kind of people who will take it upon themselves to sustain it.

In corporate America, most people will probably continue to chase the dollar. It's too bad that's the way the shareholder system is designed, because the better you treat people, the better they work. Right now you've got backlash over executive compensation and corruption scandals, plus millions of baby boomers retiring and a younger generation that expects employers to do the right thing. So our chosen method is the respected, efficient way to attract talent and run a business. Basically, it's just an organized, long-overdue return to decency.

Lance is Beryl's chief operating officer.

CHAPTER SIX:

FOCUSING ON THE CORE

B eryl got where we are today by focus. We focus on what we do in our niche and we focus on who our ideal customer is. Our services and client base have expanded, but the core business is exactly the same. Call advisors with flat screen monitors and complicated databases do exactly the same thing my brothers and I did with three-by-five cards in 1986.

We know that focus is a difficult thing for any company to maintain. If customers aren't asking you to do new things, shifts in your markets and strategies always offer tempting new opportunities. How do you address those challenges?

DEFINING WHAT YOU DO

DEPENDING ON WHERE THEY are in the chronology of their business, everybody weighs their options quite differently. In the early stages of our business, like most entrepreneurs, we were willing to look at almost every opportunity that came our way. It's smart to be flexible and open to suggestions when you're trying to get started. It's also smart to remember that nobody can do everything in a really outstanding way.

Beryl isn't an idea lab or a traditional product development company that comes up with things and hopes they work. We've never had the money to roll out radical R&D innovations and wait to see if our customers would accept them. Instead, we've always reacted to our customers and the marketplace. All our truly valuable ideas have come directly from customers. We usually had enough foresight to listen and enough patience to try what the customer was suggesting. After we were sure the concept worked, we rolled it out to other customers.

FOCUS MEANS SAYING NO

IN THE LAST CHAPTER I TALKED ABOUT our vision and our purpose of connecting people to healthcare. This is not just a slogan or a scrap of brand wizardry. It's how we make the world a better place and it keeps us focused. In new business meetings, we simply turn down jobs that don't directly connect people to healthcare.

People always ask me why Beryl only does healthcare. The reasons are simple. First, we haven't nearly maximized our opportunity in this huge market. With so much potential, why go elsewhere? The second reason is that being a niche player supports our strategy of not being a commodity business. Rather than service multiple vertical markets, our ability to focus on one area is the main reason we can position ourselves as a premium provider. Third, focus makes us the best at what we do, which earns us new business and keeps old customers loyal.

Some of Beryl's opportunities to diversify have been easier to turn down than others. The easiest were offers from psychic hotlines and phone sex companies. But I'm just as pleased we had the good sense and good business discipline to turn down legitimate non-core opportunities. Whenever we compete today against companies that don't focus on healthcare exclusively, we're already halfway home, simply because that's all we do. It brings a level of credibility we wouldn't otherwise have.

Sometimes we turn down jobs that are healthcare-related. We get offers to do work in the pharmaceutical industry, for example, which has lots of direct response needs. Every ad you see for the latest and greatest drug has an 800 number. Some company, somewhere, has to take those calls. We don't, because it's generally looked at as a business where the low price leader wins. We can't bring the same value to those companies that we bring our traditional client base.

It takes a long time before you can pick and choose the things that you do. That's not to be arrogant or to think that you're too good for other kinds of work. But if your company is at a size where you're spreading yourself too thin by doing too many things, it becomes distracting for the troops and destructive to morale. People start to question the vision and don't really understand where you're going.

When we reach thresholds like this, we start to turn business away. We formalized the process by creating a task force to scrutinize new opportunities and to come to a consensus on whether we want to get involved. The task force members have to achieve a tricky balance as they manage and defend our core focus while trying to reach our revenue goals. A company can be a little choosier once it achieves premium-provider status, but it has to keep current clients convinced that it's still flexible and open-minded.

DROPPING PRODUCTS AND SERVICES

CUTTING BACK YOUR SERVICE offerings is a much tougher call than passing on a new client. Our most radical pruning job to date was eliminating a complete product line that represented 20 percent of our revenues at the time.

We had certain clients in the managed care industry using us on an as-needed basis to support their existing call centers. Rather than let us run these operations, they'd turn to us for overflow capacity. For eight years we found this kind of work financially attractive. The projects were high volume, high revenue, and tended to pop up in the fourth quarter, which helped us make our revenue goals.

In many cases, however, the projects were also short-term, ramping up and down in six months. After a while, we decided these spikes were having a negative impact on our business. We had to let people go just months after hiring and training them, which went against our culture and values in terms of developing people long-term. Our support departments were swamped with customized projects that distracted them from their core functions. These clients also tended to want dedicated service teams, with a certain number of call advisors working their account exclusively. This completely contradicted the blended client environment that gives us scale.

Worst of all, we found out that these customers viewed us as a commodity vendor, not as a partner or a premium provider. They basically saw us a temporary staffing agency and knew that at some point they wouldn't need us any longer. No matter how well we did, they would eventually take the business back.

In 2005, our senior management team made a decision that the whole thing just went against our grain. We decided we would no longer accept this kind of business (though we retained the business we had) and agreed to tighten our focus on long-term clients who let us work their accounts in a blended environment where we can be cost-effective and pass on the savings. In 2006, we headed into our fourth quarter for the first time in a long time without that guaranteed revenue jump.

For a small company like Beryl, it's a big risk. Just the other day, we turned down a giant account because it didn't meet the new criteria. I told the team I was proud of them for making a tough call that could personally impact them in terms of reaching our short-term revenue goals. Will we have a year with less growth? Probably not, because they all agreed that the shift forces us to look ahead and focus on our core. By building the core out, we should be able to replace the old revenue many times over. Plus, there'd be no more distractions from projects that took our eye off the ball.

We know it's the right long-term goal for the company, but we've had a challenge explaining to the people impacted by the decision that this is the best move for them. We spend a lot of time encouraging them and explaining that we're just confirming our focus and that they're going to be a part of the solution. Fortified communication has helped make the whole process very healthy and cleansing.

DEFINING YOUR CUSTOMER

COMMODITY BUSINESSES TEND TO DEFINE A CLIENT as any person or company willing to pay. In the book *What Your Clients Won't Tell You*, John Gamble lays out a brilliant approach to making sure you're always working with the right clients under the right terms. A great advantage of being a premium provider is the luxury of choosing clients who fit a certain profile.

One of the surest ways to become a premium provider is to focus systematically on acquiring clients who know that relationships need to be partnerships. There needs to be accountability on both sides to make sure the long-term relationship is a winning one. The criteria Beryl developed help us make sure we contract every client under the right terms. Those new business evaluation criteria include the following:

- Healthcare industry
- Reasonable margins
- Defined deliverables
- Use of our core competency
- Right size opportunity
- Defined value proposition
- Realistic time frames for implementation
- Long-term or recurring contract
- Partner versus vendor mentality
- Client's investments of appropriate resources
- Access to people above and below our primary contacts
- Client's ability to pay
- Legitimate chance of winning the business
- We are their primary customer-interaction center

These criteria are mainstays of the "Clients for Life" training that all our client-facing people go through. We are very open with clients about this life-long ambition. We want them to know that we want to be with them long term.

Customers can help a company keep on track and love to be involved in the process. Three years ago, we established a Client Advisory Council composed of a cross section of our clients who meet with us in person twice a year. They are an informal group of advisors who tell us precisely where we need to keep our focus in every area, from executing on contracts to anticipating future market needs. They also give us direction on how we can expand our services without losing focus. This council has been exceptionally helpful in perpetuating relationships with the client members.

HASTA LA BYE-BYE

ONCE IN A VERY BLUE MOON, if you've run your business for any length of time, you will probably have to fire a client. If not as a point of principle, then for the sanity of everybody involved!

The Gamble book taught us that it's OK to fire a client or multiple clients for a variety of reasons. They might be unprofitable or unmanageable. They might treat your people poorly or require a service you don't want to provide. Whatever the reason, we found that not every relationship is for us. And when it's time to make a break, we need to have the courage to do that.

We have that choice, just as any client can choose to let us go.

Deciding to fire one of our top ten clients turned out to be a strangely constructive move. We'd been working with this multi-hospital system account for eight years before the relationship became adversarial. They felt as if we weren't providing the level of service they wanted. We felt as if they weren't engaged enough in the program to give us the ability to do our jobs right. On top of this, they weren't treating our people well.

Both of us were probably right. The question was: what were we going to do about it? I wanted to protect the revenue, but the situation was more destructive to Beryl than it was worth. After our second Beryl account executive bailed due to the stress, I had a good sense of what needed to be done, but rather than for me to make the call and then tell our team, I let them decide how we should deal with this big customer.

When the topic came up at one of our monthly business review meetings, I said, "You know what, I need your help. Here's the situation. We've had this account forever. They're worth a million bucks a year, and there's been a lot of benefit to the company. We've got eighteen months left on the contract, but we keep struggling to meet their expectations. Right or wrong, that's the perception. We've lost people, the hassle factor isn't going away and it's hurting us. Do we find a way to make this work? Or do we politely tell them to look for another option?"

The vote to fire the client was 49 to 1. The sales manager, naturally, thought we were crazy to drop an account that was driving our profits.

I got people's input and drafted a letter. We told the client in a very professional way that we had tried our best and thought they should find somebody else. We offered to give them a reasonable amount of time in which to do that and to help them transition as smoothly as possible. The client came back and said, "No way. We're going to hold you to the contract, but you certainly got our attention. And guess what? We're going to do better."

Maybe it was just a way for me to call their bluff, because I didn't really want to get sued for breaking the contract. But they did let their people know the Beryl relationship needed to work. And that's what happened. They got better and so did we, because I went back to our team and told them we were going to have to suck it up and find whatever solutions we needed to find. Today, this is a happy, loyal customer serviced by happy Beryl account representatives. In fact, we just signed them up for another renewal.

The biggest takeaway from that experience was the morale boost it gave my team when they saw that I was willing to walk away from a million dollars to protect them from a bully. I got letters from coworkers saying that I was their hero for supporting them. And that's where loyalty comes from. They were grateful that I listened to them and took their advice about what kind of customer meets our Beryl criteria. An e-mail excerpt illustrates:

Paul & Barry:

In my humble opinion, it was an awesome meeting today. What a blessing it is to work for a company where: 1) You can speak honestly and openly even when you disagree with the status quo or with the leaders' ideas; you can speak without fear of retaliation and 2) the leaders are willing to walk away from an abusive client to preserve "right client-right terms." You guys are awesome. I am so thankful for you both.

DEFINING YOUR COWORKER PROFILE

FOCUSING ON THE CORE INCLUDES FINDING the exact right people to deliver the services your customers need. The process we have for finding the right people has developed over time. At the call advisor level, we call it "hiring the heart, not the head." We're looking for people with compassion who have the behaviors we need to deliver a high level of customer service.

At the administrative staff level, our process for hiring people is so extensive that we sometimes get some raised eyebrows. It's taken a while to refine the process, but the effort has been well worth it. We're still refining to make sure that we ask all the right questions, test the right things, and have candidates meet with all the right people in advance. We're looking for a combination of skills and a cultural fit. You really need to have both.

Each position is handled a little differently. After candidates interview with HR and the hiring managers, they talk to a group of potential peers who have input in the decision. We do personality assessments to make sure that there's a match with all the people in the candidate's department. These assessments are equally useful in the post-hiring period. They alert us to hot buttons and sensitivities so we're better prepared to deal with issues down the road.

For example, if somebody comes up as a person who likes a lot of verbal recognition to validate their work, I'll go out of my way to deliver that. I need to be giving everyone recognition anyway, but if somebody needs it a little more, then I'll give them a little more. If I have a problem with someone, I'll look back on the assessment to figure out the best way to deal with them in conflict. Maybe there's a trait they exhibited that will help me. That's why we find this hiring tool so useful for helping manage the relationship on a go-forward basis.

While we're spending all this upfront time doing due diligence on the candidate, I tell them it's just as important that they do their due diligence on us. We need to fit them as much as they fit us. I want them to ask all the questions they want of me and other people to make sure they end up exactly where they want to be.

When we hired a chief operating officer for the first time, it wasn't something we took lightly or could do in a single series of interviews. I probably spent nine hours with Lance Shipp before I introduced him to anybody else in the organization. I needed to understand that we clicked and had similar philosophies and values. Because he has such an important role, I needed to be sure that he would operate the company in a manner that supported my manner; not the *same way*, but complementarily.

Then I put him through interviews with seven or eight people on the team and sent him on the road to meet with my mentors and advisors to see what they thought. All that work was important validation for me, because I had to find the person who was exactly right for the job. And it turned out to be a great choice. We don't do that with every position, but some version of that same process absolutely works.

LET MY PEOPLE GO

THERE DO COME TIMES WHEN IT'S APPARENT that someone is no longer a fit for the organization or doesn't have the skills required. Letting go of or firing a person is one of the hardest things a manager does, and I'm no exception to that. We generally never do it as quickly as we should, even when we know that it's the right thing to do.

I've learned that when you know in your gut that someone isn't going to be on your team long-term—or isn't meant to be there—you owe it to them to act and act now. As difficult as the moment in time may be, it's going to be better for everybody going forward. This person has a life to lead and a family to support. We're not being fair to them if we're holding them back from a solid career elsewhere. Generally, the coworker feels the same way. They understand and are grateful to get the chance to move on to the next stage of their life.

"Jessica" drove home for me the difficulty of letting good people go gracefully and ethically. She was an accounting manager who'd been with us ever since we opened the Texas facility, a great worker and incredibly loyal to the company. But after we hired a CFO, Beryl outgrew her talent.

My stomach was in knots all day, but when I finally went in and told her how we were going to treat her in terms of a severance package, her immediate response was a hug. This disarmed me and I felt much better about the conversation. I knew it was the right thing for both of us and that I was going to be fair and generous with her. As long as I treated her well, that's all that ultimately mattered.

TURNING AWAY GROWTH FOR GROWTH'S SAKE

WE'VE REMAINED A PREMIUM PROVIDER by sticking to our focus on quality incremental growth. A year and a half ago, we found ourselves in one of those hard-to-walk-away-from opportunities that I mentioned earlier. It's a long story, but I basically got sucked into team-pitching a job with a large HMO in New Jersey. The final competition was our team against a giant public call center company. We were holding up well in spite of the size discrepancy, and it was obvious that the decision committee realized Beryl was a special place.

The deal came down to price, and the competitor was so huge they had enough scale to offer a cheaper rate. Our bid was significantly more expensive, but I knew that if we tweaked a few things, I could probably prove the value of the extra expense and swing the deal.

The night before the final meeting, I was up way past midnight with my mind racing. It was a huge contract, and I suppose the lure of the dollar signs was the main reason I agreed to get involved in the first place. It's important to keep showing growth, but I had to weigh that fact against another reality. If we won, we'd have to build a new call center—bigger than the one we have now. Our coworker base would need to double almost overnight, so we'd have to find and hire a small army of call advisors. We'd have the shortest window imaginable to find people who met our service standards and no time to fill them with the spirit that makes our culture unique.

I kept asking myself, "Do we even want this? What's it going to do to the business if we get it?"

Looking back, there are two reasons why I'm glad—and proud—we decided not to come off our price. In retrospect, I'm sure that winning would have ruined the company. Not financially, but in terms of the strength and value of our reputation for service. But that wasn't the main reason I said no, either.

At three o'clock in the morning, sitting on the edge of my bed in this Newark hotel room, I remembered the day my brothers and I deliberately decided not to be a commodity business. Since that day, we'd built a great brand and never competed strictly on price in hundreds of winning bid situations. So at three in the morning, I looked at myself in the mirror and said, "Forget it!"

You have to have the discipline to walk away from people who won't accept your value proposition for what it is.

As we evaluate the possibility of getting into new products today, we keep our focus on quantifying value beyond price. If we can't do that, we avoid the product line. We're not going to grow just for growth's sake.

YOU CAN'T BUY YOUR REPUTATION!

THE FIRST ACQUISITION WE TOOK PART IN was when we bought the Texas call center. But that was a very simple transaction and we were already running the place. We didn't have to fuse our culture with another group, or go through staff reductions, or figure out how to leverage the two operations.

We've thought about buying other companies as a means to grow the business. Advertising agencies provide complementary services to Beryl's healthcare clients and frequently end up being our strategic partners. Since we take calls for clients that hire ad agencies to promote the phone number, why not buy an agency to gain complete control over those calls and round out a more robust service offering? On the back end, too, Customer Relationship Management (CRM) companies take the data we generate for clients and use it to reach back out to the callers with more personalized campaigns. People are always telling me Beryl should buy one of these customer relationship management firms and take over the whole process.

In the end, we always decide that it's better to keep working with these fellow service providers as partners. The chance of us finding a company in either discipline that is a culture match with us is pretty small. But the bottom line is that I don't know much about advertising or the CRM business. Since it took me twenty years to understand the intricacies of what Beryl does, I knew that buying a new company wasn't going to make me an overnight expert in a totally different field. Knowing from experience and from counsel how risky and distracting it is to stitch two companies together, we generally continue to avoid those opportunities.

Buying accounts is a different story. In 2002, we had another type of seamless integration when we acquired the accounts of a former competitor that had outsourced part of its business to us and eventually decided to drop this market niche. In 2005, we bought another competitor's accounts from the group that acquired it. Buying accounts has been a good growth technique for us. Our new customers are generally thrilled by the higher level of service and we avoid all the factors that tend to make acquisitions so difficult.

Jared's story

Before I came to Beryl I worked for another healthcare-related call center and a bank call center. Both places had really high turnover and really low morale. The workers were as miserable as the person making the call. You could feel the negative mood everywhere around you, the whole atmosphere. There was no way to advance. You were there to do phones until you quit, got fired, or died.

At Beryl, there is some place to go and people who care about my future. After I'd been a call advisor for a year I was approached by the director of operations, who is now my mentor. He saw some potential and desire, and actually approached me. He helped me recognize strengths and develop them. Equally important, he helped build up my confidence. That's real important when you know you want to do more but don't know how to get there.

For the last year and a half, I've been given a chance to work at a position that requires me to communicate directly with a portfolio of client accounts. Some of them are very big clients of the company. I really enjoy this kind of professional interaction, and I'm good at it, which surprised me a little bit at first.

After a series of events like this, for the first time in my life I feel like I'm at a place where I want to build a career. I want to create my own position, which would be a fantasy in most places. But it's not a fantasy here. We have a lot of newly created positions. As I learn more about what my strengths and talents are, I think I'll be able to find my own niche.

Having worked the phones, I know what the heart of the business is at Beryl and how important the culture is in supporting the call advisors. You can take a hundred and twenty calls in a ten-hour shift and you're going to be dealing with a lot of people who are already at their emotional breaking point the second you greet them. Everything that's important to them is tied up in that one call—their life, their money, their future.

People scream at you because their lives are falling apart. They explode when you tell them their condition is the one thing their insurance doesn't cover. The next call may be a mother who is hysterical because her child's condition keeps getting worse. You have to give her the information she needs and somehow find a way to console her. An elderly patient may just want to talk. Loneliness may be a psychological health issue for him, so you have to steer the conversation back to the business at hand in a way that makes the caller feel like he's not a nuisance or a bore. The way you handle him will make a big difference in his day and his overall outlook on life.

After a series of really emotional calls like that, it's very helpful to be able to tap into a supportive culture. The company knows what we're up against and they have a lot of ways to help us recharge our batteries.

Jared was recently promoted to customer relations manager.

CHAPTER SEVEN:

NOT A MOM-AND-POP ANYMORE

E very small company goes through changes and different stages of growth. Looking back, it's easy for me to see now, that for a long time at Beryl, we were remarkably isolated. We had great coworkers and a nice set of clients, but no real nourishing connections to the larger business world around us. We weren't used to networking or learning other ways of doing things.

Quite a few times I remember feeling frustrated and restricted by this mom-and-pop mentality. I felt that there was a real need for us to go beyond the limited knowledge we had about how to do things. Surely there were lessons to be learned if we explored outside our small circle of operations. One of my first priorities as CEO was to put together an outside network to help me tap into people and build up a knowledge base that would strengthen my leadership abilities.

HEAD OUT OF THE SAND

IT WAS A BIG EYE-OPENER FOR ME to find out that there were other business people facing the same challenges I was going through. I joined an organization of fellow CEOs that I could talk to in a support group type of environment. My interaction with these executives was so helpful I became very open to meeting any network contact that someone might make available.

I actually remember asking a lawyer I got to know, "Can you just introduce me to some business people? They can be bankers or people who've owned any kind of company. I'm willing to listen and learn." It sounds naïve, but it worked a lot better than I thought it would. I set up lunches and sat down with these people and said, "This is what we're doing at my company; this is what seems to be tripping us up. Tell me what you think."

I got so much out of these meetings. Experienced business people enjoy sharing their stories and experiences. It's rewarding for them and a great way to get free advice. I also benefited from the new people they would introduce me to. Everybody who took time to meet me would invariably give me two or three great contacts to add to the network.

VISITING CUSTOMERS

IN A SERVICE BUSINESS, the only people who can tell you what your customers need are the customers themselves. It's one thing to have them come visit your shop or have phone calls with them. It's great to have a contract and deliver on that contract. But heading out to their turf for some quality face time is what really counts.

In our case these are primarily hospitals and healthcare organizations. Traveling and listening to our main contacts and members of their team gives me a perspective I'd never get otherwise. It's part of my duty to speak to and listen to our customers, because the information they give me enables our coworkers to succeed. You can't get this information with phone calls and e-mails. Thorough debriefings are required, even if they take place in the context of an informal "social" visit. After these visits, I get very energized and immediately turn around and deliver the input to our team.

We spare no expense at promoting the idea of team members visiting customers. We may have great, hard-working coworkers who are pushing back on some of the new things our customers are asking us to do. All I have to do is put them on a plane. No matter what department they're in, they always come back as advocates of the program because they heard the same thing we told them directly from the beneficiary's mouth. Visiting with customers face-to-face has helped us outgrow the insularity that can hamper small companies.

Hayley W. (3/16/05)
Subject: L.A. Trip

Paul:
I just wanted to say thank you for the trip! It gave me even more pride in what we do here at Beryl.

BUILDING STRUCTURE

THE BIGGEST CHALLENGE WE HAVE AT BERYL TODAY is hanging onto our innovative culture as the business grows. No one can deny that as a company grows, there's a greater need for structure, accountability, discipline, and process in areas that previously were not as critical or didn't exist.

After many years as a fairly free-wheeling mom-and-pop shop, we naturally have coworkers who seem to consider the word "accountability" to be a direct threat to a fun culture. If you ask them to be more accountable, they'll accuse you of sabotaging the culture. Explaining why that's not the case will probably continue to be a challenge in the future.

One of the main points I got from *The E-Myth Revisited* by William Gerber was how the most successful companies develop a consistency in the way they deliver service to internal and external customers. When you go to McDonald's, you know exactly what's on the menu, what the food is going to look like and taste like, how much it's going to cost, and how you're going to be treated.

Businesses that want to become premium providers are well-advised to develop a similar recipe for success, a manual which, if followed, guarantees customers a consistently high-quality experience with what you sell or what you do. Don't write it in stone; continue to refine the process. Take the things that worked well when you tried them and make them absolutely repeatable as a discipline. And you can't do that without establishing some structure and accountability.

Smart people will support a formalized recipe for success, because everyone wants to be part of a successful company with a progressive culture. After the Beryl team read the Gerber book, we came up with what we call the PRISM project. This literally certifies processes across the company. More than just standard operating procedures or increased bureaucracy, people have rallied around the PRISM program because they understand the power of formalizing the program.

If you explain the process and the necessary changes properly, coworkers can make the transition from the old, less structured approach. When new coworkers sign on, they can be handed the manual and taught fresh to deliver in the same way. Without a process recipe like this and the documentation to back it up, the result is a company that works in silos and doesn't work as a cross-functional team. These problems result in low morale, low productivity and low profits. They kill long-term growth.

It's common sense to memorialize what you do well, find room for improvement, document and teach the improved approach, and make it a discipline. Consistency is what drives profit into a premium provider business.

BUILDING CROSS-FUNCTIONAL TEAMS

RIGHT AFTER WE WON THE AWARD for being one of the "Top 10 Places to Work" in the Dallas area, our leadership team also identified the silo mentality that had been building at Beryl. I thought, "Well, this is strange. I just got a fancy plaque and my name in the newspaper based on tons of happy comments from people who can't seem to play well together. What's going on?"

From my personal investigation I got the sense that there was great loyalty within the individual departments, but from a cross-functional perspective things had really started to deteriorate. I didn't have the kind of experience where I could snap my fingers and fix the dysfunction, so I sought out Dr. Larry Peters, a professor at the TCU Neeley School of Business who I'd met during my networking outreach. Larry teaches courses on managing people, so it seemed like a good place to start. I laid out the problem for him and he asked me if I wanted to let his MBA class take Beryl on as a "living" case study. They would help us try to solve our problem as part of their curriculum.

We jumped at the opportunity and I went out and spoke to these thirty-five students. I was very open, gave them the history of the company, and talked about all our issues. They then set out on a twenty-week effort to understand what was going on in the company and to bring back recommendations. Larry's students had many meetings with everybody on our team, and the class divided into three different analytical groups to make sure their evaluations squared.

The process alone was fulfilling because our people saw that we cared enough about the problem to bring in outside help. They liked the fact that the evaluators weren't trained experts or high-powered consultants, but were people just like them who worked at other companies with similar issues. Our folks shared their thoughts candidly and the teams came back with very practical, very helpful real-life solutions. To this day, we are still implementing some of the great ideas they came up with.

Can I say that there are no silos in the company today? I don't think I'll ever be able to say that. But we're a long way from where we were before, simply through an understanding of why those silos developed in the first place. Beryl was structurally restored as a result of the TCU study. It helped us create cross-functional teams with common goals. We were able to set up communication channels that allowed people to understand and appreciate what everybody here is doing *in a combined effort* to deliver service to our customers.

More than 100 of the 900 or so graduate business schools in the country have classes where students offer similar consulting. It's usually free and definitely worth investigating if you're past the start-up phase and facing issues that require high-level analysis.

THE OVERSIGHT COMMITTEE (OC)

SILOS COME FROM BREAKDOWNS IN COMMUNICATION and lack of business process. Tasking people with a job and asking them to do it is not enough. They need to understand why they're doing what they're doing and why that role is important in the bigger picture. We found out we needed to explain these things very thoroughly to each and every coworker. Once they understand their part, and how all the other parts work together, there's a sudden change in how they respect and trust others. Coworkers start talking, communicating, and sharing in the success as a group.

Committees we've established, like the OC, have improved our ability to build cross-functional teams. The OC includes representatives of each department who get together once a week to talk about ongoing issues and initiatives. The OC is the place to come and say, "I'm struggling with what's going on with your area because I'm waiting for this, and it's not being developed."

There have been lots of books written about how costly meetings are and how only "the right people" should be included. I fully believe that *nobody* should be communicating on an issue unless *everybody* who is involved in the resolution and communication of that issue is in the room. It's counterproductive to have e-mails going back and forth on a particular issue or to have two people sitting in an office with a closed door talking about someone else. The OC brings in everybody involved with the issue as soon as possible and gets it resolved. We do it with discipline and it's been a great help.

OFFICE OF PROJECT MANAGEMENT

BERYL'S OFFICE OF PROJECT MANAGEMENT takes those horizontal functions in the company that touch multiple departments and brings them together to make sure they communicate on specific pieces of work. In a way, it's the glue that holds together what otherwise would be separate functions and separate departments.

We have multiple people in this office whose responsibilities stretch across the company. They never work in a vertical way with just one particular department, so there's no perception of them playing favorites. They are responsible for—and therefore forced to work with and communicate with—all the mini-tribes that tended to pick fights with one another before we had the study done. It does a lot for the general psyche of everyone else to understand that there are impartial people in that type of mediating position.

CREATING A LEARNING ENVIRONMENT

CREATING A REAL LEARNING ENVIRONMENT helped us shake the mom-and-pop rap. It's one thing to train people in their specific job, it's another thing to help them polish and take pride in their basic intellectual gifts. I wish we had the resources and tools that larger companies do, but our internal training department has done an awful lot with what we can afford to commit.

BOOK CLUBS

AMONG THE MANY SMALL THINGS any company can do, few pay off as well as book clubs. Beryl has a voluntary club where people can sit around and drink coffee and talk about whatever book they've decided to read together. It doesn't have to be a business book, and these get-togethers have become very popular with people who hadn't previously been big readers.

I can relate, because up until a few years ago, I never saw any value in reading business books and had no interest in it myself. Once my mentors made me wade in, I found that I was picking up a lot of useful information and very specific suggestions and practical tools I could use on the job. I started reading any business book I could get my hands on and became a reading evangelist throughout the organization. Right now there are thirty books on my nightstand. They tend to stack up because we have small children that require my attention when I get home from work.

I also read multiple newspapers every morning to learn things that will help me have conversations that day, and I also cut out articles and share them with people on the team. They appreciate the fact that I'm dedicated to their learning and to helping them understand what's going on in the world, plus to showing them how it might impact and make them better.

My more proactive "involuntary book club" application targets our monthly business review meetings. As many as seventy-five coworkers get a month to read a book I've read and found impactful. Again, these are not only leaders, but representatives of all parts of the company, including call advisors. I buy copies for everybody and basically require them to submit a book report based on three or four questions I distribute. This one- or two-page report is due twenty-four hours before the next meeting. If they don't turn it in, they can't attend the meeting. This isn't seen as punitive; people would be so embarrassed if they hadn't read the book that they wouldn't show up anyway.

Sharlett M. (10/12/05)
Subject: Management Challenges

Hello Paul:
Just wanted to share with you how excited I was with the book Management Challenges of the 21st Century. *While going through this book, I was constantly amazed at the similarities between how Beryl conducts business and the identical recommendations of the author. Also, I wanted to thank you for your personal note and response. It still amazes me that a CEO would bother with us "little guys."*

You can't assign Tolstoy-sized books, and you have to throw in a few that people can breeze through in one night. I'm generally looking for concise books with quick lessons to learn. Anybody can knock out Robert Maurer's *One Small Step Can Change Your Life—The Kaizen Way* in three hours and benefit tremendously.

Every time I force my management team to apply the concepts of a practical new book to what Beryl is doing, I get at least fifty focused suggestions on how to improve the place. They have to explain how the new concepts apply to their jobs. Great practical ideas have come from these reports and discussions. If nothing else, it helps people sharpen their analytical and writing skills.

Not everybody will like all the books. After months of exasperation on his part, one coworker recently told me, "You've finally assigned a book I can relate to!" And I told him I was looking forward to our discussion. If the worst thing I do in life is help people learn, I'll take a little push-back. Most individuals welcome a chance to improve themselves.

You don't have to do a lot of research to keep a program like this running. Coworkers will start to suggest books on their own. I get suggestions from people in my network, too. Every time I send one of them a book they'll all turn me on to new titles. Just put it out there as something you're interested in, and all kinds of different sources will open up.

Lara F. (4/13/04)
Subject: Books and Miscellaneous

Paul:

Thanks for the new book; our department revised the entire filing system based on the "touch the paper on your desk only once" theory. It is now totally caught up. I will read the new one tomorrow while I am waiting for my daughter to come out of surgery.

I even send books to clients when I think it is appropriate, and rather than sending another box of muffins, I use books as my annual gift to customers during the holidays. One client recently sent me a great note that read, "Thank you for the great book. Every year your gift provides me with training in business success as well as leadership skills. What a great idea to train your partners! I can't tell you how much I appreciate your gifts. Thank you and happy holidays."

We just had a major client come through for a tour and they are now considering us for a huge contract expansion. Their representative was impressed with the display of books in the showcase downstairs. I gave him one and said, "This is basically what we're all about these days." He flipped through it and said he wanted to send me the book his boss lived and breathed by. What marketing intelligence could be better than that?

INTERNAL TRAINING

ONE MOM-AND-POP ATTRIBUTE that Beryl will never abandon is how we try to develop our people from the inside. A family-owned business like ours naturally tends to create loyalty and grow leaders within the company. We've had a great track record of doing that, but it took us a while to figure out that training doesn't happen by sending somebody to an Excel class or by bringing in a speaker to talk for half an hour.

Training is a tricky discipline for Beryl, because we get paid for people sitting in a seat, taking calls. Pulling them out of those seats and off the phones goes against our moneymaking goals. Still, we're very proactive to schedule time off for people so they can learn and be exposed to what's going on in the business. We just have to apply a lot of discipline and control the process carefully.

When we invest in people's training, we hold them accountable to execute on what they've learned. If we send somebody to a three-day seminar, I don't want to hear that they had a great time. We ask them to write a document explaining how they're going to apply the new knowledge to their situation or their team.

Lacking the right training tools and resources, we have failed at times to develop people to be the type of leaders the company needs. When good people stagnate for lack of training, a growing company essentially passes them by. This makes the loyal old co-worker look like they failed, when in reality we let them down by not giving them what they needed.

Doris R. (4/10/04)
Subject: Goodbye Is Not Necessarily Forever

Paul and Barry:
I resigned today due to the manager's inability and lack of experience to lead the department, leaving me no room to develop critical management skills to better serve Beryl. The lack of a true leader made our department the weakest link. . . . It has also created a bottleneck for Beryl to pursue and achieve its goal and vision for the future. . . . While we are strong in some areas of our business today, we are not strong enough to conquer all challenges ahead of us without passing your leadership and vision across our entire business. . . . Without that leadership in our department, we started to lose our business focus . . . And refuse changes in a competitive world . . . .

It didn't take many more e-mails like that before we said goodbye forever to Beryl's clannish mom-and-pop employment policies. We'd learned the hard way that the best salespeople, as just one example, don't always make the best sales managers. We could tell that if we kept promoting exclusively from within the company, the company was going to stagnate. We had to welcome outside talent to help us grow the company. They had knowledge we didn't have; knowledge we couldn't live without.

Our solution now is a combination of outside and inside talent. Every once in a while, our existing coworkers will question our commitment and loyalty to established coworkers, but ultimately they understand and buy into the philosophy of combination and balance. People who used to report directly to me see that as Beryl grows, I may have less time for them than I used to have. That ego hit goes away pretty quickly when they start reporting to someone with ten times more knowledge in their functional area than I ever had. Now they get to be trained and truly developed under highly-qualified outsiders. They feel fulfilled because they're actually acquiring hard new career skills that have solid value in the market.

Lali's story

I've been with Beryl for three years and it's very family-oriented compared to any other place I've ever worked. What's important to me is the culture and the way people care. I'm a cancer patient, diagnosed with cervical cancer last year. This meant that I had to miss a lot of work for treatment, which was tough for me because I'm a single mom with two children.

Beryl put together a bake sale and raised three thousand dollars to help me pay my bills. I was really surprised they collected all this money for me. After I got out of surgery and they took me to my hospital room, the first thing I saw was a big beautiful arrangement of flowers from Beryl. It meant so much to me that it made me cry.

Most companies wouldn't even send you a "get well" card. You just take calls for them and that's it. Paul himself sent me a card. Both he and Lance sent me cards when I was out. Coworkers were cleaning my house and dropping off Kentucky Fried Chicken. It's something that came from their hearts and when they see the owner doing something, they want to do the same.

That's the way they are with us. Last Tuesday, Paul and Lance served us breakfast and juices. Even though they work as hard as they do, they reach out to everybody. We're included in the decisions they make. There's no difference between them and us. It's family-based and family owned but it doesn't stop there. They let us know that we're family, too. Other places you clock in and clock out and nobody is even interested. Your day is done.

Every year we do all kinds of things like the Susan Komen Cancer Walk. We give things back to the community and I'm happy they do such things for other people. We always have spreads of food here and eating together makes us happy. We go to movies together. There's always something to keep us entertained. A lot of the things we do include family and I can bring my children in here whenever I want. My daughter knows everybody's name. When I come home from work she'll ask me, "How's Paul doing?" My whole family is happy I'm here.

Lali is a call advisor in Provider Services.

CHAPTER EIGHT:

OVERCOMING CHALLENGES

s I've tried to make clear, my brothers and I were pretty green when we first got going. With hard work and the help of good people, the business took off, in spite of our inexperience. I'm certainly a disciple of Jim Collins and the ideas in his book *Good to Great*, but the road every company has to travel on its journey from good to great is going to have some potholes in it. Beryl is no different, and we continue to face challenges managing our people and customers.

We've been very lucky that there was never any one obstacle or error that put the business seriously at risk. If someone had given us $20 million to invest in the company early on, we probably would have made far bigger and much more serious mistakes. Not having access to that kind of money, we had to grow slowly and conservatively, and most of our mistakes didn't show up as much.

Still, when you have to make a lot of decisions every day, they're not all going to be good ones. A few examples spring painfully to mind when I think back on things we wish we'd handled differently.

THE HALL OF SHAME

THE FIRST MAJOR BLUNDER WAS OUR LEASE IN LOS ANGELES. At the end of the first five years, we had two options: renew for another five or sign on for something short-term. We thought we would get a better deal by going long, but we were chosen twelve months later to build the call center in Dallas. Suddenly, we didn't need the space. We managed to sublet part of it, but ended up taking a pretty significant financial hit for the rest of the contract. It was one of those things you just kind of have to suffer through and survive. I was kicking myself because in my gut at signing time I remember thinking, "You know, there's no real reason we need to commit here, long-term."

That was a mild goof on my part compared to what happened in 1992, the year an ingenious thief hacked into our phone system and racked up a hundred thousand dollars in long distance bills. A hundred thousand dollars is a lot of money and was a very big deal for us back then, something we couldn't let slide. We felt the situation was AT&T's problem, but AT&T has clear tariffs that say their customers are responsible when thieves squirrel into their systems.

That argument didn't make any sense to us. The bills weren't ours and we didn't feel like we should be penalized because some high-tech bandit ripped us off. AT&T kept trying to collect the money and finally took us to court. To this day, that is the only lawsuit ever filed against us.

My short legal career made me feel that I could take on AT&T. I was pretty sure, actually, that I was going to kick their asses. The judge called a pre-trial conference in his chambers, and when I walked into this meeting with the other side, he looked at me and said, "*What are you thinking?* The case is black and white and you don't have a leg to stand on. You may not like that, but that's the way it is."

When we settled soon thereafter, it cost us a bit more than the original debt and the outside attorney fees I was trying to save. Those fees would have been a great investment, because those attorneys would have settled the debt earlier for a lot less.

Why did I fall victim to the same forces that made me abandon law in the first place? I knew the economics of the system always force people to settle. I knew that regardless of who's right or wrong, it's just too expensive for the little guy to keep litigating. So why didn't I do the smart thing and heed the counsel I used to give my own law clients?

Because I got carried away with principle and pride. I felt so strongly that we shouldn't be responsible for this money! Then my competitive drive kicked in, and I psyched myself up into thinking we really could win. Because I like to win, I was emotional, and maybe a little arrogant as well.

Going head to head with AT&T taught me that you can't take the world on without thinking things through, and when you need professional advice, you should seek it out. And that's the upside of these not-so-good decisions that every executive makes. Do you learn anything while you're picking up the pieces? Did the ordeals make you any better?

BAD HIRES

ALL MANAGERS MAKE BAD HIRES, but I think for the most part we've learned to choose better. We had to let one go a few years ago who reminded us that no matter how much effort you put into the process, you still may end up with egg on your face. In this case, we wanted to find a sales star with excellent experience. We used a recruiter who does tremendous due diligence and has always given us excellent results. After a long search she ended up referring a gentleman we'll call Greg.

Greg worked for a very large IT firm in healthcare and had tremendous credentials and a great personality. When he joined the company, we agreed that he could work out of his home in the Northeast. From day one, something seemed a little awry. We couldn't understand why after three or four months someone with his level of experience wasn't quite getting it. I traveled with him a couple times and everything seemed to be OK. But something wasn't connecting.

Rick, the husband of our salesperson Linda, happens to be a consultant in the healthcare industry. One night he was at a dinner party with an executive at the company we squired Greg away from. When Rick mentioned Greg's name, the other executive said that Greg still worked there. And when Linda took it upon herself to call this firm the next day and ask for Greg, sure enough, the receptionist put the call through. Voice mail picked up and said, "Hey there, this is Greg. I'm in all week so please leave me a message and I'll get back to you as soon as possible."

Mystery solved! The reason our man was proving a little slow on the uptake was because he had never left his prior employer. He was just sort of moonlighting at Beryl, long distance.

I had to go to New York the next day, so Linda told Greg to come meet us in the city and make a presentation as if he were pitching a prospect. I think she explained this to him as a training exercise. We met him in the bar upstairs at our hotel and confronted him. He couldn't deny it, and we ended up taking his laptop and Blackberry and bidding him farewell.

Naturally, we felt like morons, even though we knew we hadn't done anything wrong. Our hiring policies are pretty meticulous, but once somebody signs on, we don't call the HR department at the old place to make sure they're not still working there on the sly.

This was the only time in my career where I had to let somebody go and wasn't dreading the experience. Greg rose to the occasion by insisting he should be paid through the end of the week.

DEALING WITH A DOWN YEAR

MANAGING RISK IS A COLOSSAL CHALLENGE we came face-to-face with when we had to deal with a rare "bad" year in 2002. By virtue of the fact that we have no outside investors or an outside board of directors, one could argue that it doesn't really matter that much if we have a bad year or a bad month or a bad quarter. We can just pick up and keep going and hope that the next year is better.

On the contrary, my mentors and advisors always counsel me that if I want to build value in the company, I should show a consistent growth track record every year. There doesn't need to be a lot of growth, but there needs to be some. I've taken that very seriously as a personal goal and was disappointed in 2002 when we went down on the revenue side a couple hundred grand. Even though we were basically flat from the year before, the impact was a lot greater on our people than it was on the balance sheet.

What happened was that two very large clients concluded that through no fault of Beryl's they could take their business back in house. It was the right business decision for them, but we had a concentration problem because their percentage of business against our total revenue was high. It probably took us two years to recover from the disruption because it's so difficult to maintain the same level of profitability when revenue disappears. After taking too long to respond, we did the best we could and started to build back up.

The down-year gave us an understanding of what our business is really about and how to protect ourselves from risk. We figured out a good defensive strategy and a mechanism for minimizing volatility in the future. We came through it better focused on what we do well and more committed to our mission. Every year since then has been a record growth year.

We also learned that, whatever you do, don't sugarcoat the truth in situations like this. It's best to be honest in terms of what's going on in the business, especially with coworkers. There are always bumps in the road, and that's OK. As long as you keep leveling with your people, they'll ride along with you.

ALLOWING MISTAKES, ENCOURAGING REBIRTH

A GREAT WAY OF BRINGING COWORKERS WITH YOU is by letting them know that making mistakes is OK, too. If I can sign a bonehead lease, pick a fight with AT&T, and hire a guy like Greg, I can't very well walk around making people feel like idiots every time they drop a ball. We like people to feel comfortable and know that it's normal to make a bad call every once in a while. They're not going to be shunned or frowned upon or yelled at. They're going to be asked, "What have you learned and how are we going to do it better next time?"

Carol E. (12/21/05)
Subject: Have a Great Holiday!

Paul:

. . . You have provided us with the chance to try new things, get some of them right and some of them not so right, take responsibility, not be discouraged from trying again, and hopefully getting better in the process . . .

We encourage people to use their talents and try to make good decisions. Trust your gut if you have to, but try not to bet the farm on raw intuition. In a business like ours, which over-flows with data, there's really no need to do that. Generally, your gut is going to be right, but it's much more persuasive to back up your recommendations.

Job flexibility is another challenge we're starting to tackle more seriously. What do you do when people burn out? I've had two very senior managers proposition me recently with new roles for themselves that were not logical advances from their current positions. In both cases I felt comfortable enough to let them essentially make up new jobs for themselves.

Eric, our former director of operations, used to supervise 150 people. Now he has one direct report. My immediate temptation was to think, "Wow, how can you do this? You were at such a high level in the company." But his rebirth worked like a charm. Today he has much more energy, is learning new skills, and is using his talent to help the company achieve continued success by helping us launch new products. He is able to grow personally and contribute in new and exciting ways. The move allowed us to bring in a replacement with fresh ideas that have supercharged the operation. Look what we get out of that exchange and willingness to be open.

This rebirth concept gives a lot of hope and relief to good coworkers who might feel they've reached the limits of their talents in a particular position or department. In most corporate settings, people think they have to protect their positions at all times. They only think about moving up, never sideways or into something completely different. If they can't do that, they feel like failures.

At Beryl we are working hard to let people know it's OK to make non-traditional changes. They don't have to worry about people looking down on them if they don't take the normal course. The fact that we allow this flexibility, actually encourage it, means that people end up staying here. Rather than move them out, we might hire someone from the outside that has more experience, but we'll find another place for the established coworker and give them a renewed sense of purpose.

Eric D. (4/26/05)
Subject: Thanks

Paul:
Thanks for taking some time to get me back on track. Blind spots

can be frustrating to both parties. I really feel like I have now been able to identify what has bugged me for the last few months.

That feeling of defensiveness, the need to measure my words and cover my backside, is against my nature. It has had a physical effect on me. Your comments made things much clearer. Your trust and belief in me mean everything. I want to continue to earn that trust.

LOST IN TRANSLATION

ONE OF THE DOWNSIDES OR RISKS of having such an open culture is that you will get aggressive feedback sometimes. In fact, "back-lash" may be a better word! Last year in our ongoing communications, for example, we kept talking very enthusiastically about how the company was seeing record monthly growth and profits. Our coworkers didn't understand what this meant to them. Their attitude was, "Why aren't we seeing it? What's in it for us?"

The challenge to overcome here was translation. We had to find a better way of explaining the results of the business and what they mean to coworkers at every level. Part of the problem was that people didn't understand what they were already getting. As in most companies, our coworkers were just looking at their base salaries. To redress this we developed a "Benefits Calculator" that tallied all their pay incentive and benefits, plus some of the cultural things we do. This showed them the full picture.

We also took time to show all coworkers how the "Circle of Growth" really functions as a running cycle. We hadn't been doing a good enough job talking about the regular investments we make in the business. We quantified the investments and came up with almost $4 million that we were pumping back into the company in terms of people, technology, and other tools and resources that make everybody's job easier. This got us a much greater appreciation for what we were doing, but, again, it's not something we could just do once and hope the message would stick. We have to do it on an ongoing basis.

ENTITLEMENT MENTALITY

OUR BIGGEST CHALLENGE AT BERYL goes hand-in-hand with our greatest achievement, the creation of a fun and dynamic culture. Believe it or not, doing a lot of nice things can backfire. The worst result is when an entitlement mentality develops.

To understand how this pitfall gets set up, let's look at our morale machinery in action during a recent five-day period. The week began with "Call Advisor Appreciation Day." Everybody dressed up like Hollywood stars because the theme, fittingly enough, was "You're the stars!" Two days later, on "Movie Night," we rented a local movie tavern and had two showings of *Gridiron Gang*. Both showings were packed, and everybody yelled and screamed with pride when the Beryl screen ad we bought to recruit new coworkers came up. Everybody ate and seemed to be having a good time.

At the end of the week, we had the dedication of our new deck outside. It was kind of emotional, because they dedicated it to my brother Barry. This event ended with an ice cream making contest, which is a major sport here in Texas. In California, I never met anybody who owned an ice cream maker; here it seems like all the folks have their own ice cream machines. There were teams and contests and prizes for the best flavor, funkiest ingredients, and prettiest color.

On Saturday, quite a few people from the company ran together in a 5K. There were a lot of comments flying around about what a special and magic week we'd all shared. Everybody seemed to realize that our culture program was really exceptional. Everybody seemed to appreciate the fact that this program generates a wealth of good vibrations without which the days would drag in comparison.

The problem, obviously, is that not every week can be like that. We can only stage one sidesplitting talent show a year. Just as my brothers and I came to realize that business is not all wine and roses, our coworkers at times are challenged by the cruel fact that labor cannot by definition be a 24/7 circus of ice cream and movies. Some weeks there may not be any costumes and prizes.

Invariably, if we go two or maybe even three weeks without a jam-packed schedule of festivities, a very small group of individuals will start wondering out loud what we've done for them lately.

Our attitude is unaffected. There will always be naysayers but we will just keep doing the right thing no matter what. We're committed to make Beryl a special place to work and we try to be sensitive to everyone's needs. After a number of years, we've finally realized that we can't make everybody happy, much less keep everybody deliriously happy around the clock. No matter what we do, there will always be a few people who don't want to go with the flow. That's OK. Rather than call it ingratitude, our insightful HR team sums it up like this: "Not everybody drinks the Kool-aid."

If you adopt a dynamic culture model, some people will become a bit spoiled. It's just human nature. And, when the fun

activities take a dip, they may feel like you've changed the culture or wonder why you've taken those things away. When this
entitlement mentality kicks in, we've learned that we have to deal
with it and push back a little. It's tricky, because when you push
back even a smidgeon, some people will accuse you of becoming
hard-hearted and taking the whole thing away.

These accusations used to hurt my feelings. Now I understand
that we enabled the mentality by letting a few folks complain and
demand too much and work the system. Recently we were talking
about setting up a community program where Beryl would match
any personal donation a coworker made to a charity. I thought it
was a fabulous idea until I was warned that some people would
take advantage of it and make donations up. I didn't want to
believe that, but was assured that under a similar program we've
had coworkers try to abuse fundraisers to pay their own bills.

Another disheartening example was the "Angel Tree" we set
up on Christmas so coworkers could help each other get gifts for
their kids. One person got a lot of presents, but she didn't think
they were nice enough. That one really got under my skin. But
here's why you can't let the rare few who don't drink the Kool-aid
wreck the party for everyone else:

One of our call advisor's sons, sixteen years old, was just diagnosed with brain cancer and given a year to live. Having gone
through what I went through with my brother, I'm very familiar
with the diagnosis and came in over the weekend to talk to her
about it. I'm going to spend time with her son, and do what I can
to help him and try to make him feel more comfortable at this
hard time in his life. The company will rally around him as well
by doing things like fundraisers and whatever else makes sense.

In the back of my mind, I'm already bracing for the trouble-some handful who might say, "Well, if you're doing that for her and for him, what about me?"

It's a very tough balance. How do you pick and choose?

My position is that if we know in our hearts that it's the right thing to do, I'd rather take the risk of alienating a few than pass up an opportunity to do some real good. If you let this kind of negativity and selfishness get out of control, it will strangle any altruistic spirit you ever tried to share.

Keep passing out the Kool-aid!

JULI'S STORY

I started as a temp here four years ago. I used to work at a telephone company where we were all monitored like kids 24/7. It was so bad my manager used to follow me to the bathroom if I wanted to take a personal break. I was expected to do things I didn't agree with, like selling things to customers that didn't benefit them. We were doing what we had to do to benefit the company. Every caller you talked to was mad because he'd been waiting on hold for an hour to complain about a bill he just got for $1,000.

At Beryl, we're dealing with human beings, too, so I still get a few people who don't want to answer all the questions I may have to ask them to figure out their insurance coverage. But at least I know I'm helping them with something important. And no matter how hard the job gets, the company always has something fun going on here like the Gong Show or Customer Service Week. They make sure we know we're needed and wanted.

My family had some financial problems a while back after my husband was in the hospital for two months. We were between homes for a few weeks, and when my kids got ready to move to a new school district, the company helped out. People were always keeping in touch with me and the senior leadership always asked how my husband was doing. I've sold candles to Paul's wife and he sent me an e-mail telling me how much she and his daughter liked them. At other places where I've worked you were lucky if you could even approach your immediate supervisor.

I don't think there's anybody here who isn't treated like an individual. We have the PRIDE certificates and I like to use them a lot to recognize other coworkers. I feel like the profits are shared among the people and I find it interesting that the owners really try to work for us and not just for the company or for themselves. They didn't need to help my family and they didn't try to make it a big deal. They kept it amongst themselves because a person's privacy is a big deal here.

Juli is a call advisor in Provider Services.

CHAPTER NINE:

LESSONS LEARNED

O ne of my most successful efforts at sharing with the whole Beryl team was my series of essays on the most important lessons I'd learned about life and business. I wrote these "Top Lessons Learned" over a period of weeks in the fourth quarter of 2001 as a means of totally opening myself up and being vulnerable. A confident leader can be vulnerable and open up to coworkers.

My experience has been that the more you share and the more you let people in, the more loyalty and dedication this inspires. I met a new class of call advisors just the other day and was telling them all sorts of personal stories. I told them how I met my wife on a plane, and warned them that, whether they liked it or not, they were going to get to know my kids. They loved it.

People *want* to connect with their leader as a human being, not as the boss. I see it every day in situations like the last 5K run the company participated in. After the event I was standing around sweating with everybody else. A coworker came up and started asking me about my kids, commenting on their photos in my last monthly e-mail letter.

The basic themes of my "Top Lessons Learned" were that experience matters and we all keep learning and getting better year after year. I wanted people to review their own careers and consider whether some of the lessons I'd learned might help them achieve the goals they were planning for the year ahead. The lessons actually did inspire a lot of people, so whenever I go out to speak at MBA schools today, I usually end up going through the same list. I've even shared them with clients I've become close to.

HONESTY

MY CAUTIONARY TALE ON HONESTY IS ALL TOO HUMAN, kind of funny, and not immediately related to business. But it definitely illustrates the fact that truth is the best and only policy in any environment.

When I was living in Los Angeles, my best friend's name was Wyle. He, too, has since died from cancer, but was married at the time. My girlfriend and I were meeting Wyle and his wife for Sunday brunch at the Cheesecake Factory. A number of weeks earlier, they'd invited us to an event that I didn't really feel like attending. To get out of it, I had decided to tell Wyle I had to go to a jazz concert with my girlfriend's sister—a lie.

As we were standing in line outside the restaurant he asked my girlfriend, "So how was the jazz thing with your sister?"

She looked at him and said, "What?"

And Wyle said, "You know, when you guys went to see jazz with your sister."

And I looked at her intensely and said, "Yeah, remember? *The jazz concert?*"

My girlfriend blinked a couple times and said, "What?"

And I said, "*Remember? Jazz?* With *your sister?* The *OTHER NIGHT?*"

And she looked at me and said, "Paul, what the hell are you talking about?"

Wyle knew exactly what was happening and he was such a nice guy he just moved on to another topic. We sat through breakfast as if nothing had happened, but I was never more uncomfortable in my life. My heart was in my stomach the whole time. I had been caught in this stupid lie. Later that day, I called Wyle and told him how bad I felt about lying to such a good friend. He couldn't have been more gracious, so I'm lucky I got to learn such a critical lesson with my best friend instead of a business associate.

Personally or in business, it is absolutely *never* worth lying about anything. There's just no excuse at any level. All trust is immediately destroyed forever. From that point on, there is no way to build a relationship. Since Beryl is in the relationship business, dishonesty is a clear violation of our values.

As this book goes to press, it seems like every newspaper I read is nothing but a swirl of scandals involving corporate leaders and politicians. Hewlett-Packard executives are taking the Fifth Amendment in front of Congress while the Enron CFO heads off to do his six years in prison. What kind of profit did he gain that was worth losing everything he had? I just don't get it.

It's so much better to have a clear conscience and know that nobody can ever get you in trouble. Everybody has skeletons in

the closet, but I sleep a lot better at night knowing there's nothing in mine that can really pop up out of nowhere and bite me.
At Beryl we made doing the right thing a hard and fast policy,
not only because it's morally correct, but because it's just plain
stupid to do the wrong thing.

PERSISTENCE

I AM COMPETITIVE AND I LIKE TO WIN IN BUSINESS AND SPORTS. Most
often the challenge is more exciting than the victory, but when
we won the right to build the national call center in Texas, the
win felt great. My brother Mark and I were at breakfast with the
client when he told us we'd been chosen. We said thank you in
our most professional way and promised to do our best. Then we
walked back to our hotel room and jumped up and down on the
beds for five solid minutes.

We never would have won without persistence, because right
before we got the win, our necks were on the chopping block.
Multiple requests for proposals and changing teams of decision-
makers had dragged the process out for two years. Many times
throughout this period we were given indications that we were
the company of choice. In the very last days, we found out that a
competitor in Colorado was going to be chosen. Then Columbia
CEO Rick Scott had made a trip out to visit the competitor, and
I was told it was pretty much a done deal.

We had two choices: let that happen or do something about
it. Since the Columbia executives had never been to visit our
facility in Los Angeles, I overnighted a personal handwritten note
card to Lindy Richardson, a primary decision-maker:

Lindy:

I understand that you're coming to the end of your evaluation, and I know you're leaning toward another company. But I also know you've never been here before. After everything we've been through, I'd just like to request that—before making the decision—you take the opportunity to come and meet us and meet our people. Then I'll respect whatever decision you make.

Paul.

And it worked. The note card got her attention and she brought another decision-maker out to spend the day. After two furiously frustrating years of pitching, once they came out to see us it only took three weeks to get the contract signed. We had to fly to Nashville to meet Rick Scott ourselves. After he and I had a casual five-minute chat, he walked out and told his people, "These are the ones."

The importance of persistence is always uppermost in my mind. We currently have an opportunity for a very large potential business arrangement with a new company being founded by seven people with wonderful track records. They are targeting the consumer market in healthcare and a partnership arrangement could very well take Beryl to a whole different level.

In this situation, we got involved early enough to help their team put together pricing models for the investors. These guys have been so successful that getting the money was never a concern, but after the investors came in, the CEO called me to thank me. We arranged a day-long conference that felt a lot more to me like a launch meeting than a sales meeting. His team did not ask the questions about our technology that usually suggest we're in a run-off. So we skipped that part of the dog-and-pony show and did a lot of white-boarding instead on how Beryl could help these guys enter the market in twelve months' time.

At the end of the day, the CEO thanked us again. Then he said he'd be in touch in a couple weeks. He said he was "leaning toward" Beryl and would probably be asking us to come to their headquarters soon to work on the contract—after his team checked out one other company. The tone was all very pleasant, but when my team heard about the potential spoiler, it naturally took some air out of our balloon. Once again, we were under the impression that we were the chosen ones. Suddenly, doubt and insecurity kick in. You start thinking, "Well, what if we lose?"

So for the next couple of days I walked around wondering exactly what this prospect's parting words meant. Was he just starting his negotiating tactics by making us think we weren't the only game in town? Or, after all we'd been through, was the contract really on the line? As soon as I had that *déjà vu*, I called the CEO on his cell phone.

I left a message telling him I appreciated the visit and thought the meeting was a productive one. I told him I heard his comment about looking at someone else, and completely respected and understood. However, it made me wonder whether we'd prepared the best agenda for the meeting. Had we spent too much time on implementation? Were there technical aspects of our business we should have covered?

I was reaching out to say, "If there's anything you need as you do this evaluation, please let me know." Because, obviously, I didn't want to lose the business thinking that we hadn't put our best into the effort. And, to be honest, there was another thing I was doing with this call. I wanted some reassurance. I was pretty confident, but not about to give up. An hour later I got a call back: "Paul, don't worry, great meeting, we'll be in touch next week."

The point: if you sense the slightest element of risk, start pulling out all the stops. Reflexively, I went ahead and did this anyway. I had everybody on our side in the meeting write everybody on their side a personal thank-you. And I assume they were impressed when we overnighted these twenty-four note cards with a thick kit of diagrams and visuals and workflows that summed up the results of the discussions.

Persistence is the heart of competition.

Until you get the signed contract, stay in full-bore sales mode.

NOT BURNING BRIDGES

BEFORE HE BECAME A LAWYER, MY DAD WAS A BANKER. To this day, I still meet people who remember him from his banking days. Almost all of them describe him as a kind and genuine guy, one of the nicest people they ever worked with. I don't think I do a very good job of it, but I try to live up to his example the best I can.

Many years ago he told me, "Always be nice and never burn any bridges."

In business that's tough advice to follow. Frequently, I want to make a not-so-nice comment. Every once in a while I want to say something sharp. But the years have taught me how important it is to let go of these impulses. You never know when you may need that person or that relationship at some point in the future, perhaps many years down the road.

If you have a disagreement or a personal problem with someone, swallow your pride and drop it without any personal attacks. It just isn't worth it. When you run into these people later on down the road, they'll respect you for having maintained such a high level of professionalism.

It's a small world and Beryl operates in a relatively small niche. As corny as it may sound in an aggressive free-market economy, following my dad's advice about taking the high road has served me very well over the years.

It's always the right road.

SETTING GOALS

HERE'S ANOTHER LESSON I LEARNED LATE. Seven or eight years ago, I didn't see much value in setting goals. I knew that I worked hard and believed that hard work would make good things happen. Experience has convinced me since that without setting goals, a company and its people won't get nearly as far as they would otherwise.

As Beryl gets bigger, I've realized that the discipline at other companies is much stricter and more structured. In meetings with some of our new senior people who came from big companies, I've been amazed at the level of accountability they're used to seeing in strategic and tactical plans. At this point in Beryl's history, I think it's healthy to admit that we're much better at writing plans than holding ourselves to the outcomes.

The consequences some people face at the big companies for not making their plans are a little too severe for me. I don't really ever want to get to that level. But I also realize that we've been a little loosey-goosey. Someplace between where they are and where we are today is probably the best place for us. If we ratchet our accountability up a notch, and stick with our concept of getting a little bit better all the time, it's going to pay off.

Setting goals has certainly allowed me to achieve more. I set both personal and business goals for myself every year and track how I'm doing. It's really just to help guide me and challenge myself, and it's been very effective.

I also create a future vision for my own life, looking five years out and asking where I'd like to be at that point in time, professionally and personally. Pete Lakey, one of my mentors, taught me this. Each year I rewrite my future vision based on how I feel at that point in time. Sharing this concept also helps keep coworkers focused, as the following message shows:

Carol E. (12/30/05)
Subject: Goals

Paul:

You are right about the benefits of setting personal goals. Frankly, I've never been big on that, but have begun to understand the importance of setting them to the importance of leading the finance department.

I also read a book on the plane that inspired me to think about what went right and not-so-right over the year personally, and then set some goals. I'm still working on getting them in final form, but the process has already helped me begin to say "no" to some personal opportunities that are not the best fit for me right now, so that I can say "yes" to even better things that fit with my goals.

One really good question that the book asks is "What would you do if you could not fail at all?" Very thought provoking and great encouragement to dream big!

OPTIMISM

EVERY SITUATION WE ENCOUNTER IN OUR PERSONAL and professional lives offers us the ability to choose how we are going to react. How will focusing on the dark side of things help me succeed? I know for a fact that involvement with negative people has never helped.

It takes a sense of confidence to stay positive in the face of daily challenges, but optimism is a critical responsibility for any leader. You have access to information that other people don't have, and if they see you in a down mood, their imaginations run wild. Even if you've shared everything you know, it's essential to manifest an upbeat attitude.

In the face of challenges and bad times and controversy, it's especially important to get people to be positive about what they're doing and to believe in the outcomes your approach can create. I try not to do this to a fault so that people think it's not sincere. But I do look at the bright side and encourage them to push forward and stretch their goals a little further. I try to convince them we can get there. There's plenty of negativity in any workplace. We need to squash that wherever we can and teach people to be confident about what they're doing and what the future holds.

LISTENING

AN ACQUAINTANCE I RUN INTO SOCIALLY FROM TIME TO TIME will go on for half an hour if you ask him how he's been. At this point in our relationship, I've probably listened to twelve hours of his monologues. He never asks me how I'm doing and I suspect that if he did and if I tried to respond he wouldn't pay enough attention to make the effort worthwhile. I actually like bumping into this successful and decent guy a couple times a year. Every one-sided moment in his presence is a valuable reminder to me to keep on top of my verbal skills.

I'm not pointing fingers here. Like most people, I like to hear myself talk and need to work all the time at listening. I have one very polite and polished client, for example, who embeds little nuanced messages in her most casual remarks. These help me figure out if she's genuinely happy with the way we're handling her account, or if she's just OK with the service. Most people try to feed verbal clues like that. The quicker they get picked up, the better the chances of heading off negative situations.

At Beryl, we've profited in terms of hard dollars by listening to coworkers. We keep asking questions, letting them know we hear them, and trying to validate their feelings. We encourage coworkers to use the same techniques in their interactions with our customers, asking them sincere questions and convincing them we're honestly interested in what they have to say.

It's hard to listen to someone without forming a response in your mind until the speaker has finished. If you can break this habit at the office, you might be able to break it at home!

GRATITUDE

A FEW OF MY "TOP LESSONS LEARNED" have already been covered in earlier chapters. It's important to have mentors. It's important to stay in shape. And it's important to realize that luck plays a role in the success of many businesses. If it hadn't been for all the free PR we got for saving Elulia Newsom twenty years ago, Beryl simply wouldn't be where it is today.

Looking back at how far we've come since then—and having seen the same market break a lot of other companies along the way—it's only fitting to end with the lesson I've learned about gratitude. This is not a commonly-discussed virtue in the business world today and that's really too bad.

To give a clear sense of how I structured the "Top Lessons Learned," the full text of my e-mail on gratitude runs below. The response from our staff was extremely positive, which proves that you don't have to be a world-class prose stylist or a philosophical giant to touch your people on the emotional and spiritual levels that are so important to a vibrant culture.

Any business leader who cares enough to do so can sit down at a keyboard and serve up a little heart and humanity.

If nothing else, your people will be grateful you had the courage to try.

Paul Spiegelman (11/18/01)
Subject: Thanksgiving
As we approach the Thanksgiving holiday, it makes sense to focus on two all-important but often neglected words.

I think all of us could find a number of times in our lives when we could have or should have said "thank you" to express our appreciation and gratitude for the deeds of someone else. Gratitude also extends to those things we should simply be grateful for. Instead, we too often take things for granted.

I remember years ago when our company started getting larger and we had a growing number of coworkers. I remember how good it felt to know that we were helping support the lives of many people and their families. But I don't think I ever appreciated what really made people who work for Beryl feel special and important. I used to think it was money—that the paycheck was enough. As long as we were paying our coworkers fair wages with good benefits, we had done our part.

How wrong I was! When we finally took the time to sit down with some of our staff to listen to what made them tick, the number one thing was gratitude. They just wanted to feel like we appreciated what they did for us and for Beryl. And even though they suspected that we were grateful, they wanted to hear it. They wanted us to express it. It is human nature for everyone to get a sense of self-worth by hearing someone else thank them for a kind word or a job well done. I realized then that it was so important for our staff to hear from us directly how much we appreciate their hard work, loyalty, and dedication to Beryl.

I can't say I'm perfect at this yet, and it is something I am always working at. It is really very simple; it just means stopping for a brief minute and making someone else feel good. With the fast pace in which we all operate, it is easy to get caught up rushing to the next meeting or phone call. If I just take the time to slow down and express my appreciation for those that help contribute to my own success and happiness, I've made them happy and I feel better about myself.

This week, let's all try to stop what we're doing long enough to be grateful for what we have, and express appreciation to friends and family who care about us. After the tragic attacks on our country on September 11, 2001, we should all consider ourselves lucky to be alive, healthy, and to have jobs.

These are a few things that I am especially thankful for:

I am thankful to each and every one of you for your tireless energy and spirit. I appreciate every call you take, every client you talk to, every proposal you write, every report you generate, and every new staff member you hire. Every computer program you write, every student you train, every invoice you pay, and every extra hour you put in.

I am thankful that I have a wife who teaches me about the joy of the simple things in life.

I am thankful that I am soon going to be blessed with a little Spiegelman.

I am thankful for the miracle that my brother Barry is alive and well sixteen years after life-threatening surgery.

I'll continue to work long enough to smell the roses and realize just how much I have to be thankful for. I hope you'll do the same, especially this week. When you get together this Thanksgiving, make sure to give your kids, your parents, and your friends one extra hug—for me.

Please write back to me to share what you are most thankful for.

—Paul

MARICELA'S STORY

I've been here for eleven years and it doesn't seem that long. I started back in Los Angeles as a call advisor for eight months, and was promoted to senior advisor to work on a big new account. We had to hire 120 people, train everybody, rent a floor in an office building, and turn it into a call center. It was a madhouse and a lot of fun. I remember going to happy hour with Paul and everybody else. It was such a tight team. His mother was the company trainer and a great role model, always flawless in everything she did.

Naturally, your role changes a little as your responsibilities increase. You still hang out with your team, but as you mature and have children, you don't really do tequila shots any more. But our core value of camaraderie helps keep the personal bond strong and makes sure we treat everyone the way we'd like to be treated. Once you've come on board, you can feel the difference everywhere. And we set the stage for success upfront with our policy of hiring people for their hearts.

I've been impressed at how values like camaraderie have impacted other departments in the organization and brought up the level of awareness about how we treat people. In customer services, we tend to be warm and fuzzy anyway, but I've seen the other groups transformed. It's not a value anyone can ignore, either. I get graded on my spirit of camaraderie just like everybody else.

And that's a good thing. As you go through the day you end up asking yourself, "Am I really listening to the feedback while we're implementing this new process? Am I treating others with respect, or am I being a pain?"

A lot of things have changed since I started. We used to be in a makeshift call center looking out the windows at planes landing at LAX. Now we're in a giant sophisticated facility with a full-on training department doing what Paul's mom used to do all by herself. But the number one thing hasn't changed a bit. We still treat everyone with dignity and respect and we still value everyone's opinion.

A simple example of that is the new covered patio outside. It didn't take too many comments about how hot it gets outside in the summer and how cold it is in the winter before that patio was put into a plan and built. And when people saw this really nice patio it just reinforced for them the awareness that they are listened to carefully and their opinions do matter. Your ideas may not happen tomorrow, but if you speak up, there's a fair chance they'll get put in the plan, too.

Maricela is a customer solutions manager.

CHAPTER TEN:

"KEEP IT IN THE BIG RING!"

I wrote this book to share simple secrets that might help other leaders successfully advance their businesses. I wrote it as an appeal for old-fashioned values in the commercial arena, with a special emphasis on treating coworkers well. I wanted to make available to my coworkers, who are all my friends, and to their families, a handy survey of the Beryl story and some insights into how far we've all come in the last twenty years. Hopefully, it's a story my wife and kids, Barry's wife and kids, my brother Mark, and my parents will also enjoy.

Our company has definitely been fortunate with luck and timing. Whenever one aspect of the business was going away or slowing down, some new opportunity always ramped up. I'm amazed when I look back at how the Elulia Newsom publicity kept us from going out of business, and how quickly we were able to transition into the physician referral industry. When we sold our original emergency response company in 1994, we had no idea that less than a year later we'd win a contract from Columbia to build their national call center.

Three years after that, we somehow managed to turn the negative of the Columbia business going away into a positive by buying the assets of the center. Our ability to take on this high-capacity, high-tech facility enabled us to build out our product lines and build up our reputation and brand. Today, due in large part to favorable market conditions, Beryl has an unprecedented growth platform and a real message on how we can shape the industry.

No political party has a real answer to the cost of healthcare spiraling out of control. The current market trend—consumerism—puts more financial responsibility for healthcare on the average American. This new retail model won't work unless healthcare providers give consumers the facts they need to make smart decisions. This raises the bar for our industry to provide a positive communication experience to every customer. The retail trend will also help us grow our thought leadership arm. The entire healthcare industry will increasingly look to The Beryl Institute's evidence-based data on customers.

We've turned our commodity business into a great place to work; now we're going to change the world!

THE BEST INVESTMENT YOU CAN MAKE

THE CULTURE STRATEGY THAT MADE US NUMBER ONE is built squarely on the belief that business is really only about people. Technology enables people. Process enables people. People enable people. If you're confronted with the choice of skimping or stretching on human resource development, always stretch to maximize your people's potential. Do absolutely everything you can.

Every time I meet a new class of call advisors—the people who will soon start answering phones every day, all day—I tell them to look beyond that task to everything else that's going on in the company. I ask them to figure out how we can use every talent they've brought to the company to help us grow and to grow with us. I hate wasting talent. Why throw somebody on the phones and keep them there when they could be a manager or an IT expert or an account management person? It's our responsibility to unlock the potential of future leaders.

I had an incredible experience recently when I spent a day at Hamilton Prison in Bryan, Texas, to help with the Prison Entrepreneurship Program. The program was started two years ago by a venture capitalist to teach men getting ready for parole how to start their own businesses. In a world that usually doesn't want to give a felon a job, this can be an important survival skill.

The program recognizes that some people who end up in prison have great natural business skills. They obviously put their financial and organizational know-how to the wrong use, but that doesn't mean their talents can't bloom on the outside after they've served their time. The program puts the inmates through intensive training, and prior to release, they develop business plans around a concept that they want to turn into a way to make a living. Volunteers with MBAs help the men write their plans, and business people from across the country come to Hamilton to hear the men pitch their deals. I was fortunate enough to be on the judging panel this year.

I walked into the room and met sixty guys who had spent an average of eight to ten years in prison. One had been in for thirty years. There weren't many violent offenders and they all came across as very normal people who had a clear passion for an idea. Some were nervous up at the lectern as they went through their presentations; some were very confident. One wanted to start a beef jerky company; one wanted to make and sell leather Bible covers. There was a particularly good pitch from an African American man who wanted to develop low-cost custom homes in his old neighborhood in South Dallas. All these guys said they got a lot out of us coming to Hamilton to help them, but I got a lot more than I gave and agreed to teach a class of students who have been released and have to go through another eight months of entrepreneurial training.

What is my point? Well, with 165 graduates to date, this intensive culture program has helped twenty-five men launch their own businesses. The others are all gainfully employed, except for eight who wound up back in jail. If the normal national recidivism rate had prevailed, the number of re-arrests would be 115 men.

Properly trained and motivated, there's not much the average American can't do. I heard a few inmates give presentations who had a lot more savvy than my brothers and I when we first got started. Like them, we just had an idea and some passion. If they can muster the work ethic, if they're willing to listen and take advantage of opportunities, there's no reason they can't learn the same lessons we learned and be successful.

"KEEP DOING WHAT YOU'RE DOING AND . . ."

THE ULTIMATE SECRET OF SUCCESS AT THE BERYL COMPANIES has been the absence of ego. It was always just three brothers who enjoyed working hard together and success would never have happened without our parents, who gave us our personal values. It couldn't exist without the larger Beryl family that brings so much to me and to one another. They are the real source of our success.

We have all succeeded together in spite of the usual disappointments and the many occasions when we found ourselves second-guessing our own decisions. When things weren't going perfectly smoothly, Barry and I had a catchphrase we would always fall back on to buck each other up. If we'd lost a client, for example, and he knew I was bummed out about this, he'd turn to me and say, "Keep doing what you're doing." This was an expression of brotherly camaraderie that he and I had been throwing back and forth for decades. It was a simple message: get back on track and you'll be OK.

Barry was very passionate about cycling. He had a coach in Los Angeles and trained with a bunch of other serious cyclists. After he died, his coach framed another expression that Barry was famous for and delivered it to us. The inscription said: "Keep it in the big ring!"

The coach explained to me that "ring" is another word for the gear sprockets on a bike. If you don't want to pedal too hard, if you're not really a serious competitor, you can always shift your chain down onto the smaller sprockets and sort of hang back in the pack, working those little rings. That wasn't Barry's style. The coach said that whenever the group was out riding on the roads or training in spin class, my brother wanted to keep the pace intense and was always yelling out, "Keep it in the big ring!"

The inscription hangs on my office wall today and I'm a big disciple of the message. It means work hard, don't take the easy road, and don't be afraid of a challenge. Having watched my brother live a very vibrant and courageous life in spite of his long battle with cancer, this message is the ultimate ideal for me. It helps frame how I live, how I learn, and what I tell my coworkers. Just keep at it. Don't give up and shift down onto the little sprockets. Keep pushing. Keep it in the big ring.

Beryl has just geared up a new management team that will likely bring greater accountability and structure. To keep these changes from creating fear in an organization and disrupting our culture, we'll need to make lots of careful adjustments going forward. My own role will change as I bring greater talent into the company and focus more on what I'm good at. I'm excited because my passion for the business is greater than it's ever been. Regardless of financial results, the fact that I get to touch people's lives everyday in a positive way is really the only satisfaction I need.

We'll have to be careful picking the right partners. We get lots of great offers, but don't want to be lured into one that we're going to look back on as a mistake. The bigger a company gets, the more potential it has to make great big mistakes. I really connect to the book *Small Giants* by Bo Burlingham, who focuses on companies that chose to be great instead of big. It really validated that Beryl is on the right path.

We recently did our annual "upward evaluations," where every person in the company provides feedback on their supervisor.

Just like everybody else, I need to focus on what I can do better. I learned that I need to do a better job giving positive recognition for a job well done. I was told I need to be more direct when I have constructive criticism, that and I shouldn't worry that a person will take what I say the wrong way. I was asked to indicate more clearly which of my ideas I really want people to work on, and which ones can safely be ignored by people I have already burdened with many bad ideas. If my wife were filling out an evaluation, she would add that I need to have better balance in my life and put down the Blackberry at dinner.

Hopefully, I'll be able to make my uncles and my father proud trying to achieve what they were able to successfully achieve in their lives. As Jim Collins points out in *Good to Great*, the process of improvement is an endless road and the best companies never stop getting better. At this point in time, we don't really know what lies ahead for Beryl, but we do have a good running start and a solid track record of reinventing ourselves.

No matter how unsure the future may be, there are a few safe bets. Wherever the road takes us, we'll keep getting better. When you walk in the door at Beryl, you'll immediately sense the loyalty and commitment of our people.

And these people will still be smiling.

RHONDA'S STORY

I really, really loved my husband. We met in high school in 1975 and once we started dating you wouldn't ever see one without the other. Right before 9/11, Ernest had lost a good job when Enron folded and I'd lost my job during cutbacks at Lucent. Fortunately, we both ended up at Beryl, but it wasn't too long after that when my husband got pancreatic cancer.

He survived a whole year, not the usual six or eight months. There was pain, but most of the time he had a smile on his face. I'd drive straight from work to the VA and spend the night in the hospital. I had to miss a lot of work at Beryl and don't know how many people donated vacation time to make sure that when payroll came we had some money in our house. You don't forget things like that.

Whenever I needed something I got it. When the company found out the VA wanted to send Ernest to MD Anderson in Houston for a second opinion, they knew we couldn't afford to go and offered airline tickets, anything they could do. They even made arrangements for us to be picked up at the hospital and driven to the airport. But the Lord took him home right before we were scheduled to leave. Paul and a lot of other people came to the funeral and some of them cried louder than the family. My people kept looking at me like, "*Who are* these white people?"

I'm still getting phenomenal support today two years later, and that's been good because it definitely threw me for a loop. When you go through something like that you can become disconnected. I took two months off and for a while I didn't do anything. I never thought I'd be going back to school, but one night before Ernest passed, the strangest thing happened. All of a sudden he sat up in the bed, still asleep, and said, "Are you talking about a class or going back to school? Because I really want you to do that." Then he just lay back down. It came out of nowhere and I promised him before he died that I'd go back to school.

It wasn't an easy or inexpensive proposition, but Beryl made a way for me. They asked me what hours I needed and fixed any schedule I wanted, even knowing that someday my degree might take me someplace else. How many employers do you know that will do that? Not too many in this day and age. But Paul keeps doing things to make you succeed. He and the others know you're going through a metamorphosis. They know that everything I get from school I'm going to bring right back and use at work. I hope I can do that forever.

Winning the Spirit Award that the company gives out in Barry's honor was something I'll cherish for the rest of my life. I know there are many other coworkers going through their own serious struggles, so it meant a lot to me when everybody stood up and gave me the applause. My mom and favorite auntie were both there and it was a proud night for them, too. I'm sure they called everybody back in Caldwell, Texas, to let them know all about it.

A lot of times you don't feel like you deserve something like that until somebody comes along and continually instills it in you. That's what's really good about Beryl. It's not about company. It's about the individual as a whole. They want us to succeed as they succeed and it's not just words that rattle in the meetings. It's a whole belief system and they try really hard to get that feeling across. They're always telling us that we're good and we're great and exposing us to all kinds of different issues and learning opportunities. It's just a growing experience and it's all so sincere.

Rhonda is a consumer health call advisor and recipient of the 2006 Barry Spiegelman Spirit Award.